WOMEN'S HEALTH: STRATEGIES FOR SUPERIOR SERVICE LINE PERFORMANCE

MARY ANNE LAPPIN GRAF, BSN, MS

HCPro

Women's Health: Strategies for Superior Service Line Performance is published by HealthLeaders Media.

 5 4 3 2 1

ISBN: 978-1-60146-776-8

Mary Anne Lappin Graf, BSN, MS, Author
Carrie Vaughan, Editor
Rick Johnson, Executive Editor
Matt Cann, Group Publisher
Doug Ponte, Cover Designer
Mike Mirabello, Senior Graphic Artist
Adam Carroll, Proofreader
Matt Sharpe, Production Supervisor
Susan Darbyshire, Art Director
Jean St. Pierre, Senior Director of Operations

Arrangements can be made for quantity discounts. For more information, contact:

HCPro, Inc.
75 Sylvan Street, Suite A-101
Danvers, MA 01923
Telephone: 800/650-6787 or 781/639-1872
Fax: 800/639-8511
E-mail: *customerservice@hcpro.com*

HCPro, Inc., is the parent company of HealthLeaders Media.

Visit HCPro online at: *www.healthleadersmedia.com, www.healthleadersmedia.com/marketing, www.hcpro.com,* and *www.hcmarketplace.com.*

12/2010
21818

Contents

About the Author

Mary Anne Lappin Graf, BSN, MS

Mary Anne Lappin Graf, BSN, MS, knew she would be a nurse by age four and was an entrepreneur by age five. She graduated as a nurse, and then, as a certified nurse-midwife, was privileged to assist hundreds of mothers during birth—all experiences that shaped her life and her career in healthcare.

Graf currently has full-time responsibility for business development and marketing for women's and children's services for the seven-hospital Bon Secours Virginia Health System, the largest faith-based integrated delivery system in Virginia. Prior to joining Bon Secours as vice president for women's and children's services in 2001, Graf founded Health Care Innovations *(teamhci.com)* and HCI Market Research Group. In the 16 years HCI was Graf's full-time business, she led the firm to specialty prominence internationally in women's and children's services planning and development.

As a consultant, Graf has personally led more than 800 projects in 48 states and six countries for hospital and health system clients ranging from the nation's top academic medical centers to for-profit, nonprofit, faith-based, governmental, and nongovernmental organization hospitals in the United States and abroad.

She combines a clinical background and a personal commitment to women's health with expertise in education, organizational change, facility development, and marketing.

She and Paul John Graf were married in 1974, then almost forgot to have children. They were finally joined in their 40s by Michael and Ryan, assorted fureluting pets, and for some time even by a gender-indeterminate tarantula. Graf's personal interests include almost any type of music, the Internet (eBay® diva, social media, website construction as a hobby), swimming, water aerobics, reading, and anything Notre Dame, Irish, or Japanese. With more than 7 million lifetime airline miles, travel is also in the equation.

Acknowledgments

Many thanks to all who answered my numerous requests for information with enthusiasm, and particularly for the insights and forbearance of Martin Charns, DBA, whose organizational work I have followed for years, and Rebecca Arbuckle, MBA, MHSA, whose women's health team at Sg2 yielded invaluable data. They and others quoted in the book were unbelievably responsive to my inquiries. Not directly heard in the book, but underwriting every word with what they have taught me over the years are my incredible Health Care Innovations clients and friends worldwide. It is my privilege to have worked with each of you.

My thanks also to the Sisters of the Congregation of Bon Secours, remarkable women with a history and mission to which I immediately related, and who welcomed me home to Catholic healthcare. It is an honor to be both inspired and challenged every day by this organization and by our affiliated providers and partners in Richmond and Virginia—and particularly by those whom I am tremendously privileged to not only respect but love dearly. You know who you are!

Then there is the wonderful gang at Sam and Alison Jarrar's Daily Grind, the coffee version of the television show *Cheers* located in Short Pump, VA, where I wrote all but a few words of this book. You nurtured my body, heart, and soul, and I thank you!

The team at HealthLeaders Media has been fabulous from the start. My heartfelt thanks to each of you for putting me in an ideal position to share what I can in women's health. Finally, it takes great music to write a book (or live a life). Many thanks to the musicians whose music is behind every page of this book:

- Alternative: The Black Keys, One Republic, Mogwai
- Celtic Fusion: Phil Coulter, Enya
- Classical: Sarah Brightman, Plácido Domingo, Yo-Yo-Ma,
- Country: Kris Kristofferson, Johnny Cash, and the rest of The Highwaymen
- Japanese: Jean-Pierre Rampal
- Jazz: Kenny G, Peter Pupping
- Latino: Toni Brachi, Esteban
- New Age: Denise Young, Lorie Line, and many, many others
- Reggae: Bob Marley
- Rock: Paul Simon, Fleetwood Mac
- R&B: Roberta Flack, John Legend
- One of a kind: Nellie McKay, Dr. John, John Trudell

Dedication

This work is dedicated to Richard Ireland, arguably the father of contemporary women's service lines, who died far too early in April 2010. Richard is very much missed by all of us who were inspired by Richard and his wife, Peggie Ann, through their Snowmass Institute.

And, of course, to my parents: Harold Vincent Lappin, 1911 to 1993, the Notre Dame-educated life-long journalist and managing editor whose benevolent presence nevertheless inspired my sisters and me to never use either the verb "to lie" or "to lay" casually when he was around. He'd be pleased to know I keep trying to limit my commas. And to my truly remarkable mother, Margaret Ann McGraw Lappin, who—at age 96—continues to coordinate, update, regale, prod, and recommend thank-you notes. With my beloved sisters, Eileen and Julie, the four of us truly have remained Four Women Laughing—definitely including The Infamous Orphanage Incident!

Then there is my ever-patient husband, Paul John Graf, who has never wanted anything but my happiness, and my great kids, Michael and Ryan, who somehow grew to manhood in the blink of an eye. All of them have spent the better part of their lives waiting for me to finish something I just had to do—most recently it was this book. I love each of you more than air, and someday I'll stop working. Honest. Really.

Introduction

Service line is an organizational structure focused on the outputs, or outcomes, of care. The role of service line is to coordinate the patient's journey through services related by his or her core identity or individual healthcare needs, with the goal of achieving optimal clinical and business outcomes.

Service lines cross and connect many vertical silos of healthcare—institutions and disciplines—in a way that improves access, care continuity, and outcomes, as shown in Figure A. They are meaningful to the patient during the treatment of a disease process, or because of core identity or life stage.

FIGURE A

SERVICE LINE CONNECTS FUNCTIONAL SILOS OF HEALTHCARE

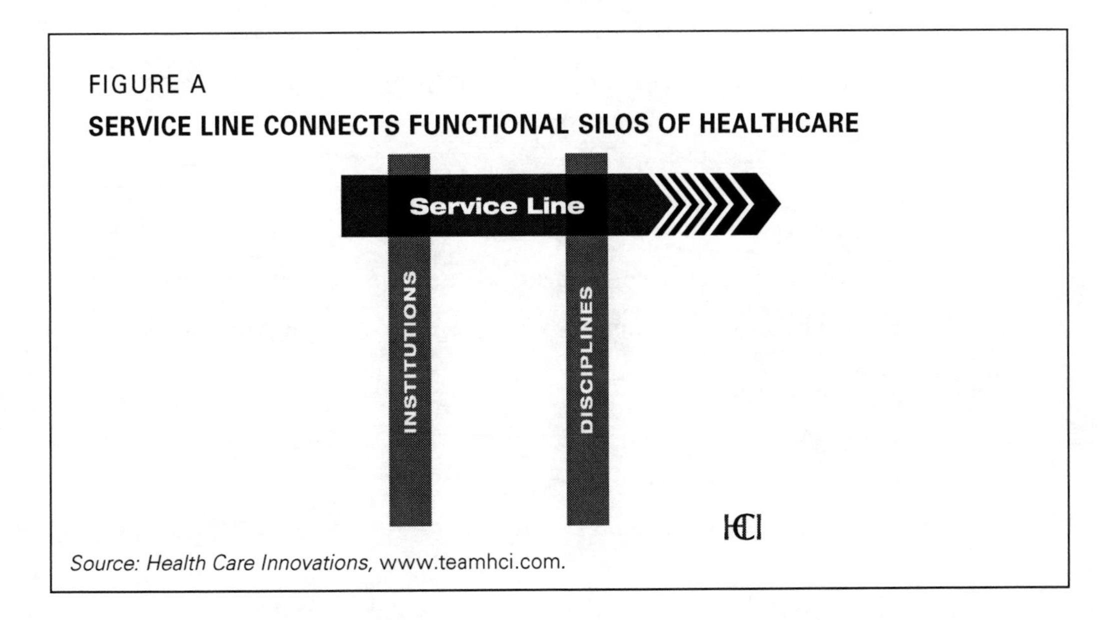

Source: Health Care Innovations, www.teamhci.com.

Service lines don't usually replace healthcare core functions, such as hospitals, departments, or professional education and development. Instead, service lines coordinate those critical functions to create value for the patient.

Service lines are implemented to yield balance and control of resources and outcomes, attract and protect key markets, and improve care of patient populations. Organizational theorist, Martin Charns, DBA, is a professor of health policy and management and co-director of the Program on Healthcare Organizational Studies at Boston University School of Public Health. Charns has researched, implemented, evaluated, and extensively published on product/service line development in industry and healthcare for more than two decades, including his most recent work on healthcare organization design and coordination (see Figure B for examples of service lines). Charns defines a service line as being:

> *Multi-disciplinary and organized around one or a combination of patient populations, a disease or family of conditions, or a technology or treatment process.*

In healthcare, services lines are also referred to as product lines, centers of excellence, clinical service lines, macro segments, core business, strategic business units, or care centers. The variety of names leads to confusion about what they really are, says Charns.

FIGURE B

SERVICE LINE ORGANIZATIONAL STRUCTURES

SERVICE LINE ORGANIZATIONAL MODELS

Disease process or condition	• Cardiovascular • Orthopedics • Cancer • Behavioral health
Populations cohorts, including core identity or life stage	• Women • Children • Men • Senior health
Technology or treatment process	• Surgery • Emergency • Transplant

To determine the organizational type or form of a company, Charns asks a series of questions, based on different forms of organizations detailed in Chapter 1. For example, one organizational form is characterized by supervisors with authority over members of a single discipline (like departments of nursing or medicine). In another organizational form, an employee may have a solid line reporting functional relationship to one supervisor and a dotted line reporting relationship to others in completely different areas of the organization. The latter form is where service line most often fits in.

Why Do Service Lines Exist?

If service lines are just a fad, they're a long-lasting one and getting stronger both in the United States and abroad. Health systems have been using service lines for nearly three decades in the United States, and service lines are even more developed in healthcare institutions in Europe and Australia, Charns says.

Service line organizational structures have a longer history outside healthcare. After World War II, the product line concept arose in the manufacturing industry, supported by the postwar economic boom and technology of the 1950s and 1960s. These product lines were developed to identify, isolate, and brand specific products. The goals were to improve strategic focus, growth, and profitability, building on the scientific base within such functional operations as engineering, finance, and marketing.

These early product lines were characterized by the emergence of science married to business leadership, and a need to grow individual businesses without totally decentralizing the functional manufacturing structure. Early leaders included the aeronautic industry and General Electric. Over the years, these firms successfully hardwired long-term success across multiple sites and disparate functions using the product line model.

Healthcare started adapting the product line concept from the manufacturing industry in the early 1980s. In healthcare, the concept was referred to as a "service" line, partly to denote the service component, and also because of an aversion within healthcare to the commercial language of "products" and "customers." The "product line" nomenclature likely caused some of the initial resistance to the service line concepts, Charns notes.

Hospitals and health systems eventually started to develop service lines as a way to better manage cost and growth.

Industry also developed product lines to ensure quality. Healthcare—paid largely for the care process, not outcomes—was slower to exercise the capability of service lines to define and derive high-quality outcomes, but this is without a doubt the challenge in service lines today—especially with the move toward accountable care organizations (ACO).

By the mid- to late 1990s, the concept of an integrated delivery system (IDS) was pushing hospitals toward system development. By 2000, service lines started evolving into a system model, rather than hospital-centric service lines, which is when it became imperative to clearly define the service line leader.

At the same time, industries outside of healthcare also made advancements in product line management. The more advanced companies have an overarching model that "strategically, tactically, and operationally integrates key functions across service lines and geographies," including cost and pricing, financing, service delivery, performance improvement, recruitment and retention, and information technology, according to Mike Nugent, coauthor of the article "Seamless Service Line Management." In many health systems, these functions are referred to as "shared services."

Nugent notes that the company leadership in these non-healthcare industries sets "clear expectations regarding functional competencies and decision-making rights/ responsibilities for each of its functional areas (e.g., revenue cycle, facilities management), service lines (e.g., neuroscience, imaging), and site-based management teams (e.g., department directors, chief operating officers, and CEOs)." By studying these companies, the healthcare industry is starting to dissipate some of the current murk around the domain of service line versus functional entities.

Currently, healthcare reform and global trends are forcing strategic prioritization systemwide in healthcare. Some of these trends include the inevitable beginning of the end of open-ended funding of healthcare, transparency of data, the recession, decrease in the availability of capital and credit, a greater emphasis on compliance, reductions in government payments, the burgeoning amount of knowledge that clinicians must be able to act on quickly, decreased utilization as consumers bear more of the burden of healthcare costs, health insurance reform, pay-for-performance, expanded insurance coverage, and the move toward ACOs. The elements all emphasize people, programs, and processes, rather than costly facility development.

Even without the current financial crisis, there is an increasing national awareness that healthcare costs are not sustainable, and our outcomes are not what they should be, given the scientific and technical capabilities of our nation.

WHAT'S THE DIFFERENCE BETWEEN A FUNCTIONAL AND A MATRIX ORGANIZATION?

BusinessDictionary.com defines matrix and functional organizations as follows:

Matrix organization

A multifunctional team structure that facilitates horizontal flow of authority, in addition to its normal (vertical) flow, by abandoning the "one person, one boss" rule of conventional organizations. Used mainly in management of large projects or product development processes, it draws employees from different functional disciplines (accounting, engineering, marketing, etc.) for assignment to a team without removing them from their respective positions. These employees report on day-to-day performance to the project or product manager, whose authority flows sideways (horizontally) across departmental boundaries.

The employees continue to report on their overall performance to the head of their department, whose authority flows downward (vertically) within his or her department. In addition to a multiple command and control structure, a matrix organization necessitates new support mechanisms, organizational culture, and behavior patterns. Developed at the U.S. National Aeronautics & Space Administration in association with its suppliers, this structure gets its name from its resemblance to a table (matrix) where every element is included in a row as well as a column.

Functional organization

A classic organizational structure where the employees are grouped hierarchically, managed through clear lines of authority, and report ultimately to one top person.

Based on the word count, it's not too hard to see which one is more complex (see Figure C for a breakdown of the differences between matrix and functional organizations). But if you're a woman with cancer, being told you had the best surgeon in the

WHAT'S THE DIFFERENCE BETWEEN A FUNCTIONAL AND A MATRIX ORGANIZATION? (CONT.)

world isn't nearly as important as being told you're cured—that is the critical difference between the functional input/process orientation of a department of surgery and the service line output/outcome orientation.

FIGURE C

DIFFERENCES BETWEEN FUNCTIONAL AND MATRIX ORGANIZATIONS

	Functional organization	Matrix organization
Organization	Vertical	Horizontal
Command and control	Singular	Multiple
Focus	Inputs, process	Outputs, outcomes
Complexity	Low	High
Example	Hospital or department	Service line

National results of service line organization show that the following three goals can be accomplished:

- Reduction in costs (and often length of stay [LOS])
- Optimal market positioning and quality
- Appropriate balancing of resources and capital

The service line organizational structure focuses on outputs or outcomes, and the functional organization focuses on inputs or processes. The need to control healthcare costs now is far higher than ever before, and service line is arguably better suited to balance cost and quality than the functional organizational structure is.

Are Service Lines Here to Stay?

There have been two earlier waves of service line development in healthcare, each taking about a decade. We are now in the third wave. The good news is that each stage has taken the best of the prior wave and built on it.

The first wave was in the '80s and was primarily built around financial analysis of diagnosis-related groups. The second wave featured marketing and business development more prominently. The current wave is around quality.

Each wave has been accompanied by a different type of service line leader, from the "super managers" of the '80s to the executive directors in the '90s and early 2000s. The latter stage often went awry and became purely a marketing ploy. For example, this was the phase when many labor and delivery staff found a new sign on the door one morning, announcing it was now a "birthing center." Processes and outcomes often stayed the same; only the name changed.

Tension often shows up between the functional side of an IDS and service lines. Those tensions may arise at high levels in the organization when capital or significant resources are in play, and at lower levels in the organization when managers have difficulty with the concept of responsibility to more than one supervisor. I asked Dr. Charns whether the tension ultimately might undermine service line as an organizational structure.

His answer was that, if anything, service line in healthcare is strengthening in the United States and even stronger in other countries. "You can expect heightened tension any time there are people who know and focus on the process, and people are added who focus on outcomes," says Charns. "At some juncture there is conflict. The conflict is always there, under the surface, it's just not articulated and managed—so you may think there isn't any, but it's just not being managed. At some point you have to manage it to mature and grow the organization."

Executives who sponsor service lines are well aware of this dynamic, and consider the pushback from each side to be part of the team learning process during change.

Ask any senior IDS executive with long-term service line experience, and you'll hear sentiments similar to those of Peter J. Bernard, who has implemented service lines in three health systems. Bernard is the CEO of Virginia's fourth largest IDS—Bon Secours Virginia Health System—which has seven hospitals, a medical group and multiple entities, and campuses throughout central and southeastern Virginia. Bernard says unequivocally that "without a doubt, service line has been a huge part of our success. I want the [functional entity] CEOs waking up in the morning thinking about nothing but their organizations, and I want the service line VPs waking up in the morning thinking about nothing but their service lines across the system. Between the two approaches, we have both the depth and breadth we need to succeed."

Are There Objective Measures of Service Line Success?

Where else do you buy just the process, not the outcome? Granted, not all healthcare outcomes are cures—but the patient and family still want the best possible outcome, and that's something healthcare has had trouble identifying and consistently producing.

With a smile easily detected through the phone, Charns notes that after his first foray into hospitals two decades ago, he came out saying, "They couldn't have organized it that way—it doesn't make sense." He says he satisfied that question intellectually with the realization that hospitals were originally organized around medical education, not the needs or wants of the patient. But the latter is where healthcare is rapidly headed now.

Examples of service line outcomes measures include:

- The Veteran's Health Administration reorganized care for 10 diseases/conditions around an "output-oriented approach to quality improvement... resulting in dramatic improvements in quality of care," according to Joseph Francis in his article, "QUERI II: The Next Generation." VHA cites improved prevention, diagnosis, treatment, and patient compliance, as well as decreased readmission.

- Judith Westphal, a nationally respected nursing thought leader at the University of Wisconsin, reported service line results include an 8% decline in unit costs per admission, improved quality of care, and rapid response to environmental change.

- The Health Care Advisory Board, a national hospital think tank, notes that "hospitals and health systems that have invested in developing and enhancing orthopedic services through comprehensive centers of excellence see performance improvements across multiple dimensions: better market share and higher volumes, but also enhanced patient and physician satisfaction, improved clinical outcomes, and increased efficiency."

- After the University of Wisconsin instituted their first three service lines, the medical center reported the following results on pre- and post-service line outcomes, according to Turnipseed, Frangou, Westphal, and others:
  - Variable but steady growth in patient volumes, enhanced market share, positive net margins, and improved patient satisfaction

- Offsetting of consistent downward pressure on reimbursement by improved patient care efficiency (LOS, enhanced preferred provider status, market share)

- Scorecard quality measures that show enhanced teaching and research opportunities

- Increased patient satisfaction scores

The Fit of Service Line With Today's Challenges

The current version of service line responds directly to today's knowledge-based economy, includes quality and bottom line performance measures, and directs operations in a competitive manner. Today's service lines meld strategy, business development, and marketing with the science of specialty healthcare.

Service line executives develop service line–specific business and marketing plans, determine where and how scarce resources should be invested, and ensure that the care delivery process itself is of high quality. This strategic dimension yields a systems-thinking perspective and a powerful management direction orientation.

The most significant vector influencing service line development in the past decade has undoubtedly been the change in orientation from hospital-centric to a system-wide scope.

CASE STUDY

Shift to systemwide service line model

In 2006, Memorial Hermann Health System (MHHS) in Houston shifted to a model where its service lines operated as one program with multiple sites capable of attracting a particular mix of new and existing patients through a variety of old and new tactics, wrote Mike Nugent in an article on seamless service line management. The organization needed to balance system resources and recognized that the old tactics of "recruit a physician and grow" or of "build it and they will come" no longer worked. Coordination across facilities was required to optimize future investment.

MHHS needed to allocate resources while responding with more agility to, and freeing up resources for, competitive challenges and opportunities. As a result of the shift in focus, the system:

- Combined redundant services set up originally by independently functioning member hospitals
- Recruited several key specialists to round out system service line offerings
- Employed systemwide service line executives
- Set systemwide clinical service line standards (e.g., for cancer treatment)
- Experienced "multimillion-dollar revenue cycle enhancements"

Today's service line leader has accountability across the healthcare system for the following:

- Strategy and business development, and marketing
- Responsibility for the patient experience across all consumer contacts with the system, from the distribution of healthcare information and promotion, through prevention and diagnosis, through the physician enterprise and care within the system, through home care and return to optimal function.
- Envisioning and garnering engagement around quality and operational performance over time and the patient care experience, as well as setting the goals and the bars for measurement.

Successful service lines also serve as the innovation hub for interrelated clinical business research and development, which is the catalyst for successful market launches of clinical and service innovation, the center of resource coordination and allocation, and the driver of overall quality of care and user satisfaction. Today, health systems usually have five to seven key service lines—more than that can reflect a lack of focus.

During the past decade, many departments—seeing the shift in organizational resources to service lines—developed "service line envy." But organizations should focus on strengths rather trying to develop service lines around all of their offerings. Service lines should cross departmental lines, focus on outcomes, and connect patient care, either for a disease process or through a core identity or life stage, spanning a horizontal period in a patient's life (see Figure D for service line characteristics).

FIGURE D

CHARACTERISTICS OF SERVICE LINES TODAY

- **Market-driven:** Organization around the patient's needs, experience, and outcomes over time.
- **Coordinated care over time:** Focused on more than a single visit or episode of care.
- **Interdisciplinary:** Collaboration with multiple related clinical and business disciplines.
- **Integrative:** Connection of the healthcare silos of institutions, disciplines, and departments.
- **Outcome-driven:** Engaged to envision and achieve desired clinical and business outcomes.

Departments such as surgery and emergency play a crucial role in many health systems, and hospitals all have departments that are critical for value as differentiating niche or that generate margin that must be protected. Often, these departments will benefit from systemwide management and expertise, and can be marketed successfully as niche department services. Examples are minimally invasive surgery centers, emergency departments, transport or transplant services, and mission services in a faith-based hospital. Often, health systems differentiate these departments as centers of excellence, rather than service lines. Whatever the name, they can benefit from systemwide management and support, and often can be marketed as a niche service to the community.

Summary

- Multidisciplinary service lines cut across traditional functional healthcare organizations—like hospitals and disciplines—to focus on outcomes of healthcare.
- Service line is a commonsense approach used for almost a century in industry and coming of age in healthcare. In fact, service line looks more and more like a requisite structure to achieve today's expected outcomes and the next stages of IDS development.
- With a well-developed service line, expect quicker responses to environmental and competitive change, improved clinical and business outcomes, and enhanced patient and physician satisfaction.

REFERENCES

Bauer, Mark, McGreevy, Thomas, Chirico-Post, Jeannette, "Establishing a Function-Based Mental Health Service Line in a VA Medical Center." *Psychiatric Services* 51:1307–1309, October 2000.

Charns DBA, Martin P, Interviews with author, 2010.

Charns, MP and Young, GJ, "Organization Design and Coordination." Chapter 3 in Burns, LR, Bradley, EH, and Weiner, BJ (eds) *Shortell and Kaluzny's Healthcare Management: Organization, Design, and Behavior*. Delmar Publishing, 2010.

Francis, Joseph, "QUERI II: The Next Generation." *Forum*, August 2006. VA Health Services Research & Development Service.

Frangou, Christina. "Hospital Profits From Service-Line Business Model." *Annals of Surgery* 33(10) (October 2008), Anesthesiology News.

The Health Care Advisory Board, "The Future of Orthopedics: Strategic Forecast and Investment Blueprint," The Advisory Board Company, 2008.

Nugent, Mike, Nolan, Kevin, Brown, Frank, Rogers, Stephanie, "Seamless Service Line Management," *Health Care Financial Management* (May 2008).

Turnipseed, William D., Lund, Dennis P., and Sollenberger, Donna. "Product Line Development: A Strategy for Clinical Success in Academic Centers." *Annals of Surgery* 246(4) (October 2008): 585–590; discussion 590–592.

Westphal, Judith, "Resilient Organizations: Matrix Model and Service Line Management," *Journal of Nursing Administration* 35 (2005): 414–419.

CHAPTER 1

The Air We Breathe

The healthcare environment is going through a seismic shift. Whether you have had service lines for a while or are new to the concept, determining how this new healthcare landscape will affect your organization and your leadership role is imperative—and context is everything.

In the course of a busy day, the context in which we deliver healthcare becomes the air we breathe—we don't notice it or have the time to consider it, but ultimately, the context will drive everything we plan or do.

The National Context

I am not a healthcare economist or a policy wonk, and you don't need to be either to effectively manage a very successful service line. But being aware of the global issues and connecting the dots on key healthcare macro-trends will help you accurately analyze your environment and predict the future trends that will impact your service line.

There are three basic categories of macro-trends driving the national healthcare discussion both in the United States and in many other countries:

- **Populations.** This category can be defined as all of the individuals of one group in a given area, including many subsets that are important in healthcare planning such as epidemiology, utilization, demographics, and psychographics.

- **Economics.** This category includes the megatrends within healthcare as well as outside of healthcare—particularly the worldwide economic slump. The impacts of increased costs (e.g., capital and technology) and decreased revenues are included here.

- **Policy.** While policy is often a result of both general and healthcare-specific factors, governments and other entities can drive policies that prompt a response, such as the current movement toward accountable care organizations.

State of affairs

Within healthcare organizations, institutions, disciplines, and service lines, movement in these three macro-trends impacts everything we do from a planning and caregiving perspective. The following is a brief overview of the current state of affairs.

Populations

It's impossible to ignore the impact of 80 million baby boomers—about 25% of the total U.S. population—in healthcare. The oldest boomers turn 65 in 2011.

There have never been so many people in one demographic segment, and boomers are going to live a very long time—longer than any other generation in the history of the United States.

The baby boom was a worldwide phenomenon after World War II, and many European and Asian countries are dealing with the same demographics. A look at the lopsided population in Japan, for instance, gives us another lens to consider the impact of boomers on a population. While Japan has socio-economic forces both similar and dissimilar to ours, the fertility rate there now is 1.21 children per woman—well below the population replacement rate, which is two children per woman. In the United States, there are indications that fertility rate may be declining as well (a concept discussed further in Chapter 4). As in Japan, the trend is a result of the economy and the increase in the number of women giving birth to their first child at an older age. Bottom line: In Japan, the aging boomer populations is predicted to overwhelm the next generation of healthcare workers. As a country, we may now be headed in the same direction.

Similarly, healthcare organizations cannot ignore the impact of around 40 to 50 million previously underinsured and uninsured Americans who will have access to care beginning in 2011 as a result of the Patient Protection and Affordable Care Act (PPACA) of 2010, commonly referred to as "healthcare reform."

Together, these groups, which are also predicted to be high utilizers of healthcare, represent roughly one-third of the U.S. population of about 310 million. Pair that with expectations of care, life-prolonging technologies, and a greater overall life expectancy, and the increased demands placed on the healthcare system may be more than the system can support.

Economics

The United States is in the midst of costly long-term war. We are currently struggling with a down economy. And we are predicted to be in world and economic distress for at least another 10 years, according to William Strauss and Neil Howe, who have five centuries of proof for their theories about a recurrent cycle of generations. They refer to this point in this century as a “crisis turning.”

The United States also has the highest healthcare costs of any civilized nation—estimated at a staggering 17.6% of the gross domestic product (GDP) in 2009 (see Figure 1.1). While the rate of growth in the healthcare sector as a percent of GDP has slowed in the past 10 years, the portion of the GDP consumed remains higher than other countries by a factor of almost double.

Hospital costs represent the bulk of healthcare costs in the U.S., putting hospital costs squarely in the bulls eye of payment cuts (categories of U.S. healthcare spending are illustrated in Figure 1.2).

PERFECT STORM

Starting in 2011, the first of the baby boomer population reaches the age of 65; at the same time, roughly 40 to 50 million uninsured patients start being able to access healthcare as a result of healthcare reform. Together, they represent more than one-third of the total U.S. population. These two groups—combined with the already escalating cost of healthcare and the down economy—present a potentially seismic change in how we do business.

FIGURE 1.1

NATIONAL HEALTH SPENDING AS A PERCENTAGE OF THE GDP

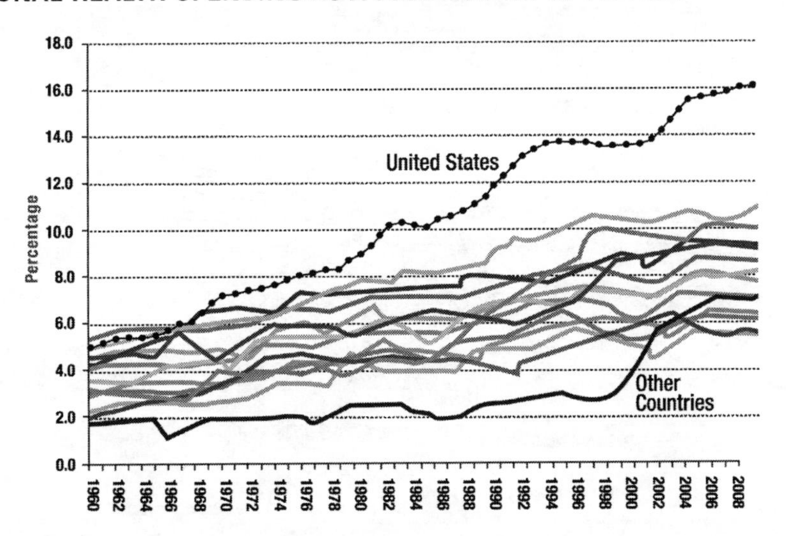

Other countries include: Austrailia, Canada, Finland, Greece, Ireland, Korea, Netherlands, Poland, Spain, Turkey, Austria, Czech Republic, France, Hungary, Italy, Luxembourg, New Zealand, Portugal, Sweden, United Kingdom, Belgium, Denmark, Germany, Iceland, Japan, Mexico, Norway, Slovak Republic and Switzerland.

Source: Organization for Economic Cooperation and Development.

FIGURE 1.2

CATEGORIES OF HEALTHCARE SPENDING, U.S.

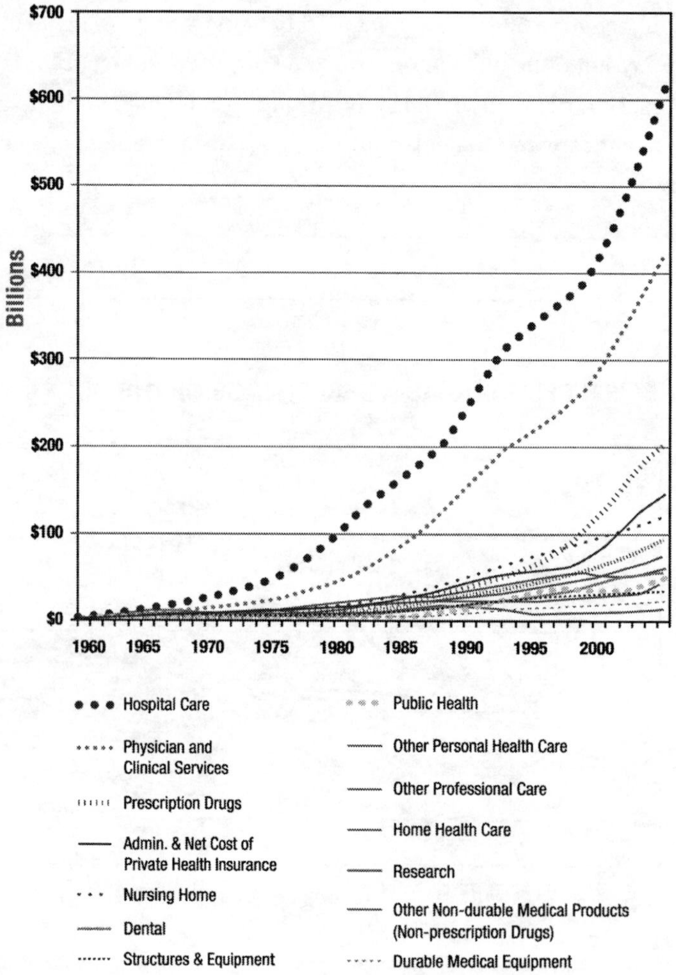

Billions

$700
$600
$500
$400
$300
$200
$100
$0

1960 1965 1970 1975 1980 1985 1990 1995 2000

Hospital Care
Physician and Clinical Services
Prescription Drugs
Admin. & Net Cost of Private Health Insurance
Nursing Home
Dental
Structures & Equipment
Public Health
Other Personal Health Care
Other Professional Care
Home Health Care
Research
Other Non-durable Medical Products (Non-prescription Drugs)
Durable Medical Equipment

Source: University of South Carolina, Arnold School of Public Health, 2008.

At the same time, the United States falls short of other civilized countries in some of the most basic measures of a nation's health. One example is infant mortality, where the U.S. rate is worse than 43 other countries (see Figure 1.3).

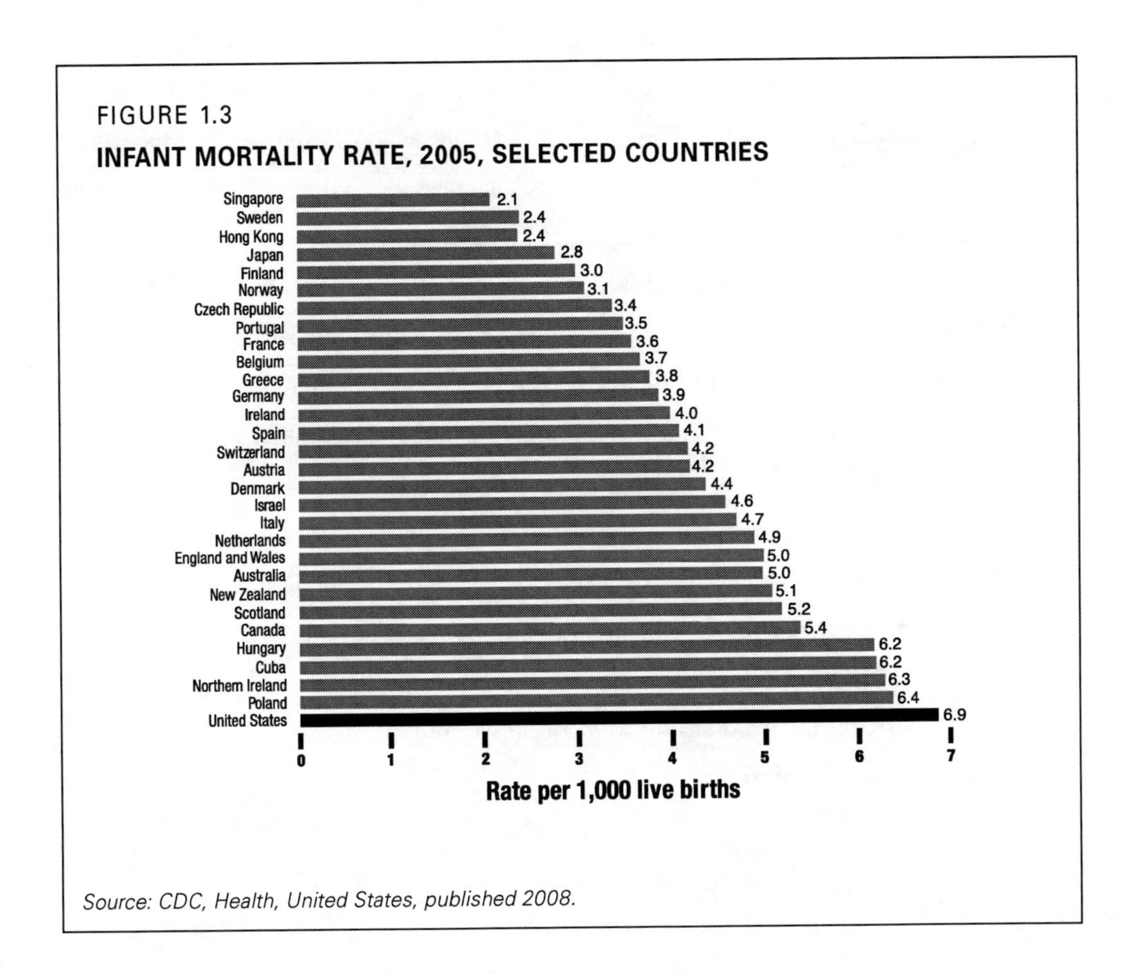

Source: CDC, Health, United States, published 2008.

Policy

Although no one knows for sure where the ship will finally dock, it's been obvious from the beginning of the 2008 campaign that President Obama ranks healthcare as one of the nation's top priorities. His leadership group has included people with extraordinary backgrounds on healthcare issues, such as Peter Orszag and deficit-balancing Jacob Lew. The passage of the PPACA—barely 14 months into the Obama administration—was another clear message that healthcare is a priority. It is likely the most significant healthcare legislation in decades. President Obama appointed Donald Berwick as administrator of the Centers for Medicare & Medicaid Services (CMS), reaffirming his plans to significantly restructure the healthcare system. Berwick, a pediatrician by training, is the founder of the Institute for Healthcare Improvement, a leading force in healthcare quality and process improvement—a direction we can expect him to continue at CMS.

The challenges are evident: The economy is troubled and rising healthcare costs continue to cause heartburn for the public, employers, payers, and providers. The last time this happened, in the 1970s, HMOs were the result—although the potential impact of HMOs at the time was congressionally mitigated by passing any willing provider legislation.

In fact, the stages of managed care in the '70s and '80s describe changes eerily similar to the disruption and reorganization we are seeing now in healthcare.

One key difference today from the managed-care era is the push for electronic health records (EHR) and the advancement of digital infrastructure in the healthcare industry. However, EHR implementation costs for one integrated delivery system (IDS) can be hundreds of millions of dollars, and there are mixed views on whether these systems actually yield savings for the health system. Healthcare futurist Jeff Goldsmith notes, "Right now, it takes remarkable imagination to find actual provider-level operating savings from installation of clinical IT." Some organizations are already using an IT infrastructure to significantly lower costs and improve quality, but most healthcare organizations are still reeling from the cost and implementation of EHRs.

Following Everett Rogers' theory of diffusion of innovations, EHRs are between the early-majority adopters and the later majority, with about 50% market penetration. Considering the technology improvements that will be made during those later stages of adoption, it's easy to assume that what we are seeing now in EHRs is nothing like what we will see in a few years. But we'll never realize those benefits if we don't go through the process of automating healthcare.

Adding those EHR costs and the necessary timeline for implementation and improvements to an already unstable healthcare economy sets the stage for the new pressures and policies we will see in the future.

What does all of this mean for women's health?

There is no need to despair at all of the challenges impacting healthcare today; there is a silver lining—especially in women's health. No one questions that the woman is the healthcare gatekeeper for the family. So far, service line leaders have viewed that gatekeeper role as a way to acquire new patients. But now, in an era of laser focus on quality, costs, and unnecessary utilization, that same family gatekeeper will also be the key to meeting these new health system goals.

You're in the right field. The service line that led to the discovery of reaching women as the gatekeepers for revenue now also has the opportunity to lead in reaching and engaging the gatekeeper for unnecessary healthcare spending as well.

The Organizational Context

It's impossible to talk about the women's health service line without talking about service lines in general. Where you and your organization are in terms of the major change from a functional organization to a service line organizational model is absolutely critical in understanding your role and—more importantly—where your organization should be going with service lines. The latter plays a key role in building your professional credibility, and also in watching for danger signs. Both should be part of a service line leader's professional toolbox.

Martin Charns notes that the only difference between a product line and a service line is the sector of the economy in which the organization operates. Both product and service lines are specific examples of a general program organizational forms, or organizational structures.

In 1993, Charns and Laura J. Smith Tewksbury identified nine organization forms or types found in industry. Charns stresses that these are not developmental stages but that any of these organizational forms can be found in organizations.

Charns and Tewksbury describe the stages, or forms, generally as follows. Note that the first eight stages are seen in both healthcare and other industry segments.

Charns says that the ninth stage, although common in other industries, is theoretically possible but unlikely in healthcare. As you read about these stages, consider where you are now and what your next stage is likely to be.

As organizations re-examine their organizational structure, it will be critical to carefully balance the benefits gained from the integration across disciplines with the benefits gained from like professionals interacting within their divisions.

STAGES OF DEVELOPMENT: WHERE IS YOUR ORGANIZATION?

1: Traditional functional organization

This represents what we commonly refer to as the unconnected "silos" of healthcare. Examples are hospitals and the professional disciplines (e.g., department of OB/GYN or department of radiology).

2 and 3: Integrator

Integrators represent the first organizational attempts to cross institutions, disciplines, or departments. Examples are often in marketing or analytics—for instance, when finance first analyzed diagnosis-related groups together back in the 1980s. In marketing, an example is marketing packaging (only) of comprehensive women's care versus just obstetrics.

4: Multidisciplinary task forces

Multidisciplinary task forces emerge when members from different departments and/or disciplines come together to form or change programs or services. They are temporary and disband after the project is completed. A multidisciplinary task force might come together to start neonatal transport services or to discover ways to decrease costs associated with deliveries.

5: Reorganized of departments (services)

In this stage, key departments are restructured to correspond to service lines. Marketing or finance may assign particular staff to the women's service line, or geneticists who are particularly interested or skilled at maternal-fetal medicine or breast-related genetics might be assigned to the women's service line. This stage starts to formalize the matrix structure for the first time, as reporting lines remain within the functional department, but a formal matrix report to the service is established.

6: Multidisciplinary clinical and management teams

This stage occurs when permanent multidisciplinary team assignments are made. While there are still formal reporting lines to professional departments—marketing,

STAGES OF DEVELOPMENT: WHERE IS YOUR ORGANIZATION? (CONT.)

finance, pediatrics—the service line executive is the team leader and now also has input into the performance evaluation of members of the service line team.

One difference between industry and healthcare structures emerges here in terms of service line leadership. Charns says that only healthcare has service lines managed by dyads or triads—two or three managers (he's also seen teams of four leading a service line). Dyads are often from the clinical and business areas. Triads are often a physician, a nurse, and an administrator. In industry, you could take a young manager with a general management background and immerse that manager in two or three disciplines for a period of time so the manager could learn more about the functional disciplines involved in a service line, but in healthcare you can't do that because the manager really can't do nursing or perform surgery, explains Charns. There are issues of licensure, for instance. "Dyads and triads are pretty powerful ways to put together a leadership team. Of course, you get new issues: getting the team to get along," he says.

Finally, if the team was more oriented toward marketing before, this is when a strengthened clinical focus emerges.

7: Matrix organization

Now the vertical organization and the horizontal service line organization become balanced and coexist, although not always peacefully. While the forms were changing, the organization was bringing together the importance of process (functional forms) *and* outcomes or outputs.

8: Reorganization into modified service line divisions, maintaining discipline leaders

In this stage, the focus shifts to the service line being primary. Few departments remain outside the service lines. Disciplines like nursing and medicine are reassigned to service lines, but still maintain discipline leaders. An example of this is a heart center

STAGES OF DEVELOPMENT: WHERE IS YOUR ORGANIZATION? (CONT.)

or orthopedic hospital in which all departments are organized to support a facility that is actually a service line.

The complexity of disciplines within healthcare makes this stage less clear-cut than within other industry sectors, says Charns. Nursing councils—essentially functional structures—still exist to link facilities and support professional nursing. Medicine and other healthcare professions need the continuing education, research, and development that typically occur within a functional discipline. Charns says it is a balance: The gain for service line cannot completely override the loss from like professionals interacting within a discipline. At some point in healthcare, the loss of the latter can become too great to balance the gain in integration.

9: Fully implemented service lines in a divisional structure

While this form is found routinely outside of healthcare, this is where Charns notes healthcare differs. Fully implementing service lines with removal of all functional institutions and disciplines is "theoretically possible," he says, but "just not pragmatic in a hospital or integrated healthcare delivery system."

"It is one thing in General Electric Company where a product line involves three or four disciplines, but hospitals have multiple disciplines, all with ongoing professional development needs," he notes. "At GE, the jet engineer isn't interacting with the appliance engineer across divisions, so that benefit is lost, but the gain is higher than the loss. Every service line in hospitals has multiple professional disciplines. In healthcare, there are too many disciplines involved, and too much to lose, if hospitals reorganize completely into service lines."

Summary

If you look at the overall trends, five conclusions arise:

1. Economics and policy are driving healthcare integration or development of what we are calling integrated delivery systems.

2. The IDS is itself at least a matrix-level model, with both functional institutions and departments as well as cross-IDS services, and IDS development parallels service line adaptation in healthcare.

3. Service line may not be the only model that works in the IDS environment, but some outcome-focused model is critical for the changes being demanded by economics and policy.

4. The functional organizational model in healthcare is quickly being integrated with service line, just as it has long been in non-healthcare industry. Healthcare can only achieve the dramatic changes required only through an output-focused model, combined with continual focus on process improvement.

5. As noted by Charns in the Introduction, any time an outcome focus (quality and cost) is overlaid on a process focus (the disciplines and institutions of healthcare), conflict ensues. Successful management of that conflict is critical to establish new, effective organizations well-positioned for the future.

References

Burns, Lawton R., Bazzoli, Gloria J., Dynan, Linda, and Wholey, Douglas R. "Managed Care, Market States, and Integrated Delivery Systems: Is There a Relationship?" *Health Affairs* 16 (1997): 204–218.

Central Intelligence Agency. "Country Comparison: Infant Mortality Rate." *The World Factbook* (est. 2010). *www.cia.gov/library/publications/the-world-factbook/rankorder/2091rank.html.*

Central Intelligence Agency. "Total Fertility Rate." *The World Factbook* (updated February 2010). *https://www.cia.gov/library/publications/the-world-factbook/fields/2127.html.*

Charns DBA, Martin P. Private interview with author, July 2010.

Charns, Martin P., and Tewksbury, Laura J. Smith. *Collaborative Management in Health Care: Implementing the Integrative Organization.* San Francisco: Jossey-Bass, 1993.

Goldsmith, Jeff. "Peter Orszag: A Powerful New Health Policy Voice at OMB." Health Affairs Blog, February 9, 2009. *http://healthaffairs.org/blog/2009/02/09/peter-orszag-a-powerful-new-health-policy-voice-at-omb.*

Passel, Jeffrey S. and Cohn, D'Vera, Pew Research Center, "U.S. Unauthorized Immigration Flows Are Down Sharply Since Mid-Decade," *Pew Research Center Publications*, Sept 2010. *http://pewresearch.org/pubs/1714/annual-inflow-unauthorized-immigrants-united-states-decline.*

Rogers, Everett M. *Diffusions of Innovation*, 5th Edition. New York: Free Press, 2003. (First published in 1962.)

Strauss, William, and Howe, Neil. *The Fourth Turning.* New York: Broadway Books, 1977. Also see *www.fourthturning.com.*

CHAPTER 2

Why a Women's Service Line?

The previous chapters examined the health care environment and the reasons why that environment calls for service line. But why should organizations invest in a women's service line in particular? Here are five reasons:

1. There is unprecedented growth in particular segments of women's healthcare, along with an avalanche of innovation in treatment and technology.

2. Women live longer than men and directly utilize slightly more healthcare than men.

3. Women direct at least 80% of all healthcare decisions for spouses, children, and aging parents.

4. Women actively seek healthcare information and can therefore be reached more easily than men.

5. And if that isn't enough, women likely present the largest untapped healthcare donor source in the United States today.

The Return of the Babies

As recently as 2007, the United States broke a 50-year-old record for the number of births. Birth rates, which were flat during the 1990s, started edging up around 2000 and were projected to increase at about 3% per year through 2020—a much better rate than in the '90s. Then the recession hit, and by 2008, births suddenly declined nationwide nearly 2%—representing a 5% budget hit for many hospitals when the expected 3% positive became a 2% negative.

But the reality is that the last children of the baby boomer generation, born in the 1970s and 80s (Generation X), are facing a biological alarm clock that can't be stopped. As the recession lessens, births will increase again—and may already be doing so. That increase will continue through 2020.

Unprecedented Growth

Boomers

About six generations of women and men are alive today in the United States, from newborns to the oldest Americans. However, one out of four is a baby boomer, and in that group is a key healthcare consumer—the baby boomer woman.

Born between 1946 and 1964, boomer women are the "sandwich generation," controlling or guiding their healthcare and that of their children and aging parents, as well as their spouse's healthcare, and often his parents'.

The boomer woman grew up at a unique time in society, during an optimistic post-World War II expansion and intense industrial development in chemistry and other sciences and technology. Medical specialties were evolving rapidly.

In the '60s, the boomer woman experienced the first reliable birth control in the history of the world—oral contraceptives. She learned medicine wasn't necessarily on her side, with examples from heavily anesthetized/medicated births and high doses of oral contraceptives that "wouldn't hurt you"—and later did—to dire warnings about how social drugs would kill you—but usually didn't.

The boomer woman is the most educated woman in the history of the United States, and the first to enter the work force in high numbers. Recently, she learned that much of her medical treatments over the years were designed for men, not women, with heart disease diagnosis and treatment being a prime example. Neither she nor her friends were that surprised; after all, they did learn from their business experience.

In short, the boomer woman is educated, experienced, savvy, and cynical—and she expects treatments and technology far more than the generation of women before her. She is about to need, and demand, technology and treatments for a host of illnesses she has never experienced before, from bad joints to gastro-intestinal problems to pelvic floor issues to heart disease and stroke. And, as it has in the generations since her birth, healthcare will reinvent itself and provide great new treatment options.

As a result, the female healthcare customer is more important to healthcare institutions than ever before.

Seniors

As the baby boomers age, we are looking at the largest percentage of seniors (as a percent of the population) ever experienced in our nation's history. The oldest boomers turn 65 in 2011. They will encounter major life changes in the years ahead, such as retirement, death of a spouse, and the personal and family challenges of aging. As they have during every life stage, boomers will change "maturity"—a phrase they are already fighting. Boomers will, for instance, rewrite death and dying—just as they rewrote birthing in the '60s and '70s.

They will also have the longest life expectancy of any prior generation—and the highest expectations of healthcare.

The previously uninsured

The Patient Protection and Affordable Care Act of 2010 opened the door for healthcare access to millions of Americans. As these populations filter into the healthcare system during the coming decade, integration of the more than 40 million new users will change the way healthcare is managed. In these families, women will likely be making the healthcare decisions.

Technology

For longer than we like to admit, medical research has been based on men's symptoms, diagnosis, and treatment. Women were essentially viewed as just like men, but "atypical." As we have learned in heart disease—the poster child for gender errors in symptoms, diagnosis, and treatment—that meant providers and women alike spent decades looking for the wrong symptoms, with delayed or incorrect diagnosis and treatment.

Gender-based research on women's healthcare issues is now rapidly catching up. The technology advances being made in areas such as urogynecology are astounding. Science is also catching up, and an array of new technology is changing the face of women's healthcare almost overnight—from fetal diagnostics to gender-based diagnosis and treatment of common illnesses. All of these changes will influence design of the women's service line.

Utilization

Women utilize more healthcare than men do at most ages—not just during their reproductive years. Women of all ages accounted for 60% of all expenses for care at physician offices, according to 2004 statistics from The Department of Labor. The Agency for Healthcare Research and Quality (AHRQ) released its most recent data in 2007, which mirrored prior reports saying that women represent 60% of all hospitalizations. When ill, women also tend to seek care earlier than men.

While about one out of five female hospital admissions was for pregnancy and childbirth, after excluding those admissions, women's admissions (18.2 million) still exceeded men's (16.2 million), according to AHRQ and other hospital data. Some of this is probably due to life expectancy, since healthcare utilization increases with age. Historically, women have lived longer than men worldwide, and the difference in the United States is currently just over five years.

WOMEN'S HEALTH STATISTICS

- Approximately 81% of women age 18–64 [about 90 million women] had health insurance in 2005. (U.S. Department of Labor)
- Women make approximately 80% of healthcare decisions for their families and are more likely to be the caregivers when a family member falls ill. (U.S. Department of Labor)
- Women utilize more healthcare than men, in part because of their need for reproductive services. Females of all ages accounted for 60% of all expenses incurred at doctors' offices in 2004. (U.S. Department of Labor)
- On average, women live six to eight years longer than men globally. (World Health Organization)
- The difference between male and female life expectancy in the United States was 5.1 years in 2006, a slight increase from the 2005 gap of 5.0 years. (U.S. Department of Health and Human Services)

The Family Healthcare Gatekeeper

A women's health service line opens the door to every service your organization offers. Women control the selection of medical services, much like they do just about any other family purchase, from clothes and shoes to food and health insurance.

Health insurance companies know who makes the decisions. A decade ago, BlueCross BlueShield launched a national ad campaign aimed squarely at women as the healthcare gatekeepers for the family: female health benefits executives, employed women, and female decision-makers at home.

In her 2010 book, *Influence—How Women's Economic Power Will Transform the World*, Maddy Dychtwald walks us through the rapidly growing influence of women as the nation and the world change. Dychtwald notes that more than 80% of healthcare decisions are made by women, and they make an even higher proportion of healthcare-related decisions, such as the purchase of 93% of over-the-counter medications. When her spouse or children are ill, at the end of the day, the woman is the one expected to comfort and care.

Women seek healthcare information

In addition to being the family healthcare gatekeeper, women are also easier to reach with information about healthcare options. Women seek healthcare information more than men do.

Women have always sought information, sometimes to the consternation of providers. More than one internist, focused on productivity, has admitted to me that he or she prefers to see men—who don't ask questions—rather than women, who do.

For example, the dramatic change in birthing of the '60s and '70s was brought about by women questioning a birth process that excluded husbands and relied on massive doses of analgesia and general anesthesia, resulting in routine resuscitation of the newborn.

Before the Internet, women sought information in magazines, newspapers, seminars, libraries, providers, and from their friends.

Once Internet searches became user-friendly, women switched en masse to the Internet, and are now the largest users of the Internet for health research—90.1% of women 25 to 34 years old (prime childbearing age) search for health information online. Half of the women in a Harris Interactive online survey say they research the Internet before even seeing a provider. The Internet has almost—but not quite—replaced family and friends as resources for healthcare information.

Because women focus on information, earlier diagnosis, and prevention, they are easier to reach than men and also easier to attract with new healthcare offerings. Ken Goldberg, MD, the founder of the first male health center in the United States, says women are just more comfortable with the language of healthcare.

It may be even simpler. Rob Becker, in his one-person play, *Defending the Caveman,* essentially reduces it to "men hunt and women gather." *Caveman*—entering its 20th year and holding Broadway's longest running solo play record—certainly strikes a chord worldwide with male and female audiences alike.

Bottom line: Women gather information.

While that propensity to seek information has been used primarily in the past to acquire the woman as a loyal patient, that same information-seeking behavior may help the healthcare industry reduce redundant costs and improve the quality of healthcare. Female healthcare consumers will be a critical key to success in the coming decade of changing priorities and goals in healthcare from fee-for-service to a more outcomes-based model of care delivery.

Potential for Philanthropy

Historically, healthcare and healthcare philanthropy has always been focused on the male VIP patient, the power player, and potential philanthropist.

In 2005, a Gallup study indicated that women control $5 trillion in U.S. business—more than the entire economy of Japan. Gallup also found that women influence some 80% of consumer spending nationally. In 2004, the IRS found that 43% of wealth holders—with gross assets of $1.5 million or more—were women, and that women had a higher ratio of assets to debt than men did. In addition, 35% of the top female wealth holders were between the ages of 50 and 65.

Women live longer than men—and widows inherit. But it's not just inheritance. The *Women of Wealth* study by Prince and Grove interviewed more than 700 wealthy women, each with at least $3 million in investable assets. Through corporate employment, 61% accumulated the fortune—their own, a family business, or a professional practice. Only 39% inherited the money, and the number of wealthy women increased by 68% from 1996 to 1998, compared with an increase of 36% for men over the same period.

The Women's Philanthropy Institute at the Center on Philanthropy at Indiana University recently published an update of their earlier 2007 study. *The Women Give 2010* study examined single men and single women to determine if there are gender differences on giving, Findings indicate that, in all income groups, women are more likely to give than men. In four of the five groups, women also donated more than men do—sometimes twice as much. At the top income quintile, 96% of women in the study were likely to give compared with 76% for men. Earlier Institute research also found that women are more likely than men to give to provide basic needs or for healthcare.

MassMutual Financial Services®, which has won national attention for its research on women's financial planning, backs up its women's initiatives with the following data:

- Women earn $1 trillion annually and are the primary breadwinners in one-third of all marriages.
- Women are involved in 80% of all financial decisions and will assume 90% of all assets.
- High-net-worth women account for 39% of the country's top wealth earners; 2.5 million of them have combined assets of $4.2 trillion.
- Women professionals and executives—1.3 million of them—earn more than $100,000 annually.

All this leads one to question the traditional healthcare view of the typical VIP patient with the potential for philanthropy, long viewed as male. The findings of banking and other industries suggests that VIP is just as likely to be a woman—maybe more so, and the primary motivator behind the male donor is often his wife. Whether from outliving (and inheriting from) a man or because she is in the

40% of high-net-worth women who earned their money themselves, developing relationships with women will be critical for those healthcare organizations that are looking at new sources of philanthropy.

These women should be engaged now not just as potential patients, but as key decision influencers and potential donors. A women's service line is your key to engaging these women, earning their trust, and putting your organization first in line for donations.

Summary

- There is a growing recognition in retail that women make or strongly influence the purchasing decisions for just about everything, from food to cars to life insurance to vacations and homes. However, traditional industries like banking and healthcare have been slower to recognize and capitalize on this reality.
- In healthcare, women direct more than 80% of provider and facility decisions. Yet women are still treated like a niche market when, in actuality, they are really *the* market.
- While women themselves use slightly more healthcare services than men, the question is not so much who is being cared for as who got them there to be cared for. Both data and anecdotal information indicate the answer to that question is more likely to be a woman than a man.

- Demographics, science, and sociology seem aligned to create a new frontier in women's healthcare, with unprecedented access, utilization, and innovation in the coming decade.

- Because women actively seek healthcare information, they can be reached more easily than men—an asset a women's service line enables the organization to realize.

- While the focus has been on reaching families for healthcare via the woman, new opportunities are emerging to leverage the woman to help decrease unnecessary utilization and lower healthcare costs, and to gain access to a largely untapped, and affluent, female donor source.

- Women are attracted to healthcare providers differently than men, and most women—66%—say healthcare doesn't know how to find them. Opening that door is the challenge of the women's service line.

References

Agency for Healthcare Research and Quality. *Healthcare Cost and Utilization Project Facts and Figures: Statistics on Hospital-Based Care in the United States.* 2007, March 2010.

Arora, Raksha, and Saad, Lydia. "Marketing to Mass Affluent Women." *Gallup Management Journal* (March 2005).

Barletta, Marti. *Prime Time Women: How to Win the Hearts, Minds and Business of Boomer Big Spenders.* Chicago: Kaplan Publishing, 2007.

Barletta, Marti. *Marketing to Women: How to Understand, Reach, and Increase Your Share of the World's Largest Market Segment.* Chicago: Kaplan Publishing, 2006.

Becker, Bob. *Defending the Caveman. www.cavemania.com.*

Burst Media. "Nine of 10 Women Online Seek Health Info Via Web." September 2007. *www.marketingcharts.com/interactive/nine-of-10-women-online-seek-health-info-via-web-1656.*

Dolan, Pamela Lewis. "Internet First Choice for Many Women Seeking Medical Information." *American Medical News* (April 2010). *www.ama-assn.org/amednews/2010/04/26/bisb0426.htm.*

Dychtwald, Maddy, and Larson, Christine. *Influence—How Women's Economic Power Will Transform the World.* New York: Hyperion, 2010.

Forooha, Rana. "The Richer Sex." *Newsweek* (June 13, 2010). *www.newsweek.com/2010/06/13/the-richer-sex.html.*

Grove, Hannah Shaw, and Prince, Russ Alan. "Women of Wealth." *Financial Advisor* (July-September 2003).

IRS. Personal Wealth Tables. 2004. *www.irs.gov/taxstats/article/0,,id=185880,00.html.*

Massachusetts Mutual Life Insurance Co. "Women's Work: MassMutual's Directive to Bring More Women Into Financial Services Is Changing How Women Look at the Industry, and Vice Versa." *Best's Review* (online) (April 2007).

Women's Philanthropy Institute. *Women Give 2010.* Center on Philanthropy at Indiana University, 2010.

CHAPTER 3

What About Men's Health?

One question that I am asked repeatedly is, "Why not a men's health service line?" Having been married to a man for a very long time, I admit to some bias on this issue. Regardless of age, many women share a similar angst: Men are less interested in inquiring about health issues than in insisting, "It's nothing, I'm fine," despite crashing to the floor while attempting to walk, lumps the size of New Jersey, bones jutting out at odd angles, or gushing blood—all hinting at possible ill health.

With that disclaimer, I'm going to attempt to stay objective by quoting serious authors on this issue and sticking to the research.

Historical Perspective

Men are not known as avid seekers of health information or care. Author Adam Voiland's articles in *U.S. News & World Report,* which combine statistics with the requisite personal perspective, confirm this reputation. "Many of us consider watching what we eat unmanly," he says. "We glorify risk taking; we drink and drive at staggering rates; we avoid screening tests like the plague; and we suppress and ignore illness as long as we possibly can. Why? Well, we're men. That's just what we do. My dad does it; so do I."

Historically, there has been a lack of interest in men's health issues—both from a personal and national perspective. For instance:

- More than one-third of 1000 male respondents admitted that they wait "until they are extremely sick" before seeking help, according to a 2007 American Academy of Family Physicians (AAFP) study. (Keep in mind that's how many *admitted* it.)

- Men are 30% more likely than women to be hospitalized for preventable conditions such as congestive heart failure and diabetic complications, according to a recent Agency for Healthcare Research and Quality report.

- Every session of Congress since at least 1999 has proposed a Men's Health Act. All seven proposed bills died, including the most recent one in 2009. That 2009 bill (HR 2115, 111th Congress) tried adding "Family" to its name, but it still didn't pass. Consigned to the House Subcommittee on Energy and Commerce the day it was introduced, the bill would have established a U.S. Department of Health and Human Services (HHS) Office of Men's Health. That was April 27, 2009. The bill hasn't been heard from since.

However, there are similarities to the emergence of women's health awareness, roughly 20 years ago, that are starting to show up in men's health. For example, men's health articles are featuring discussions long held only in back rooms. Men's health issues, for now, are also centered almost exclusively on sexuality, which is where women's health was 20 years ago. Once quaintly referred to as problems "down there" by women, the topics covered anything ovarian, vaginal, cervical, uterine, urinary, or sexual. For men, the topics being covered right now are anything testicular, penile, prostatic, or sexual.

The covers of men's health magazines today appear singularly focused on physical appearance, which was also the dominant state of women's health advice 20–30 years ago. Likewise, the formula for talking about men's health requires humor to take on sensitive issues, and strange terms emerge to avoid uncomfortable language. For instance, ads about "a going problem" are curiously reminiscent of "down there."

Growing Interest

There is a growing body of evidence that men are seeking health information online. In addition, the healthcare industry is also trying to reach out to men, as evidenced by the following:

- HHS now has men's health Web pages, with a growing body of gender-specific information for men.
- Health insurance companies are offering gender-specific health information for men and women.

- Mehmet C. Oz, MD, a cardiac surgeon and talk show host for *The Dr. Oz Show*, has a men's health section on his website. In 2009, Dr. Oz discussed men's health issues during an entire episode of *The Oprah Winfrey Show*, declaring the show a "no-embarrassment zone" for the sold-out all-male audience, including a men-only crew.

- While women are still more likely to seek personal health information online than men, the percentage of men using the Internet to seek information about personal health information doubled from 2001 to 2007, from just fewer than 14% in 2001 to almost 28% in 2007, according to the Center for Studying Health System Change.

- Three out of four male respondents used online sites for health information, according to a marketing survey by Burst Research of overall utilization of the Internet for health information reports. Generally, the younger demographics used the Internet more than older adults. But in the 65-and-above age group, more men (79%) used the Internet for healthcare information than women (77%), suggesting that men may be catching up in an age group where retirement and increasing health issues could bring both time to surf and the motivation to do so.

- *Men's Health* magazine describes itself as the fastest growing men's magazine in America. The American edition of the magazine is reportedly read by nearly 11 million men and women each month. Its online site is in the top 20 health content sites on the Internet.

However, there is a common thread throughout much of these data—the information seeking is still being done or prompted by women. While there was a sold-out crowd of men for the Oprah show with Dr. Oz, Oprah herself took the women who accompanied—or brought—the men off to a separate room for a private chat. At the bottom of the Centers for Disease Control and Prevention (CDC) men's health home page, in about a four-point font, there is this note: "Content source: CDC Office of Women's Health."

Data are omnipresent regarding the ways women direct and inform men's health. For instance, the same 2007 AAFP survey referenced earlier found 78% of men who do visit a physician were prodded to do so by their spouse or significant other. Perhaps that is a learned behavior from childhood, when their mothers made their pediatric appointments for them. Men's embarrassment during health visits may also be programmed from then as well.

None of these findings surprise Ken Goldberg, MD, who introduced the nation's first men's health center, The Male Health Center, in Dallas more than 20 years ago. Goldberg cared for men from all over the world before he closed the facility due to family illness. The Center website, *www.malehealthcenter.com*, remains a resource, receiving more than 21,000 hits every month.

The website also has a "For Women" section, since women often schedule or bring men in for healthcare appointments and are the caretakers of the men—fathers, sons, and spouses—throughout their lives, Goldberg notes. He says that men's conditions influence the women who love them often as much as those conditions affect the men. He cites the examples of impotence and sexually transmitted diseases to infertility, conception, and pregnancy to cancer, disability, and death. It's not just the health of a beloved partner, spouse, or son that is at risk; it is the woman's mental and physical health as well.

Even as pre-teens, girls have to learn the language of healthcare, says Goldberg. Regardless of whether they want to, girls (as the ones who bear the brunt of the consequences) have to learn about menstruation, conception, pregnancy, and sexually transmitted disease. Prevention is the focus. That learning continues into early adulthood, with conversations about family planning, fertility, pregnancy, birth, postdelivery care, and lactation. Pregnancy is all about healthy living and avoiding complications. After birth, women are still usually the most involved with their child or children's care, becoming even more familiar with healthcare. And, again, pediatric care is largely about prevention and early detection.

At the same time, young men are often learning about cars, Goldberg says. As a result, by adulthood, women are more comfortable asking questions in a clinician's office, and men are more comfortable communicating at the garage about car repairs. Many women don't want to know the details of what or where a carburetor is—they just want it fixed. This is similar to men's communications during physician appointments: Skip the details, just fix it.

Goldberg says that women ask an average of four questions during a medical appointment, while men ask none. His staff can tell when a woman has prompted the man before a visit, because the man comes with a list of questions. Sound familiar?

So what about a men's health service line? While men's time may be coming, for now the way to a man's health is still very much through women.

Attract the woman, bring in the man.

References

Agency for Healthcare Research and Quality, HHS. "Men Shy Away From Routine Medical Appointments." *AHRQ News and Numbers* (June 16, 2010). *www.ahrq.gov/news/nn/nn061610.htm.*

American Academy of Family Physicians. "Men Could Do Better When It Comes to Managing Their Health." *AAFP News* (June 2007).

Burst Research, 2007, as reported on *www.marketingcharts.com/interactive/nine-of-10-women-online-seek-health-info-via-web-1656/burst-media-health-information-internet-use-by-age-genderjpg.*

Center for Studying Health System Change. "Adult Information-Seeking About Personal Health Concerns, 2001 and 2007." Tracking Report #20. *www.hschange.org/CONTENT/1006/SP1.htm.*

Goldberg MD, Kenneth A. *How Men Can Live As Long As Women: Seven Steps to a Longer and Better Life.* New York: Summit Publishing Group, 1994.

Goldberg MD, Kenneth A. (Ed.). *The Men's Health Longevity Program: A 12-Week Plan to Bolster Your Health, Get Lean, Boost Your Brainpower, Power Up, Feel Great Now and Later, and Keep the Sex Hot.* New York: Rodale, 2001.

Goldberg MD, Kenneth A. Private interview with author. July 2010.

Goldberg MD, Kenneth A., and Schoonmaker, David. *When the Man You Love Won't Take Care of His Health.* Racine: Golden Books Pub Co., 1998.

HHS/CDC men's website: *www.cdc.gov/men.*

Oz, Mehmet. *http://ask.doctoroz.com/topic/mens-health.*

Voiland, Adam. "7 Reasons Men Die First." *U.S. News & World Report* (June 13, 2008). *http://health.usnews.com/health-news/blogs/on-men/2008/06/13/7-reasons-men-die-first.html.*

Voiland, Adam. "Why Men Are So Good at Dying." *U.S. News & World Report* (March 13, 2008). *http://health.usnews.com/health-news/blogs/on-men/2008/3/14/why-men-are-so-good-at-dying.html.*

Woodson, Cheryl E. *To Survive Care Giving: A Daughter's Experience, A Doctor's Advice on Finding Hope, Help and Health.* West Conshohocken: Infinity Publishing, 2007.

CHAPTER 4

Key Trends Driving Women's Health Programming

The megatrends that are driving change in healthcare overall are establishing the direction for women's services as well.

In healthcare, we're dealing with the following:

- More healthcare system development across the entire care continuum, generally aimed at being and potentially qualifying as an accountable care organization.
- Continued alignment with physicians, whether through engagement tactics with voluntary staff, such as relationship development and legal financial arrangements, or through employment.
- Decreased access to capital—for at least the next few years—and an even longer-lasting impetus to do more with less.
- Increased investment in technology, often with a high price tag, forcing organizational prioritization of investments.

- Government and payer-driven focus on improving quality and decreasing costs.
- Increased need for mission-driven services—due, in part, to the economy. The hope is there will be a shift in non-reimbursed care as expanded coverage kicks in from the Patient Protection and Affordable Care Act of 2010.

These are the forces driving clinical and business strategy in women's health service lines for the next decade.

Although "women's health" has long translated to obstetrics and gynecology, women only have an average of two children and perhaps one hysterectomy to give to obstetrics and gynecology. The remainder of a woman's life goes far beyond their reproductive system. In fact, the specialty of internal medicine makes the argument that the true women's health providers are internists.

Still, obstetrics and often neonatology play a significant role in most hospitals. Pregnancy, childbirth, and infants account for just under 24% of all hospital discharges. This includes the baby—birth itself is around 12% of all hospital discharges. In fact, seven of the top 10 hospital procedures in 2006 were associated with giving birth and newborns. And among all hospital procedures performed on all patients 18 to 44 years of age in 2003, 44% were related to pregnancy and childbirth. High-acuity neonatal units generate a substantial margin—often greater than cardiology on a per-occupied-bed basis. Obstetrics, as an art and a science, is rich in data, well confined in terms of variables, and relatively easy to study and report on.

Finally, other market factors being equal, in my experience, if a hospital has attempted obstetrics and been unsuccessful, that hospital is unlikely to be successful in any other developmental focus on women's health. Whatever people, program, or process issues prevented success in obstetrics will interfere with development of other women's programs. Because of the role of obstetrics in successful women's service lines, trends in this arena are important for planning.

Obstetrics and Neonatal Care

Births from 2000 to 2020 were originally projected to increase 2%–3% per year as the daughters of baby boomers came fully into their childbearing years. From 2000 to 2007 that held true, offsetting the relatively flat birth rate of the 1990s. In fact, 2007 was a record-setting year, and from 2012 through 2020, the number of births each year was originally projected to be the highest ever achieved in U.S. history.

Then the recession hit.

Of all working demographics, couples of childbearing age are the most economically vulnerable in a recession. Despite the increase in pregnancy among older women, the *average* age of U.S. mothers at the birth of their first child is 25. These young families have an average gross family income of $45,000 or less per year at the time of pregnancy. They have disposable diapers, not disposable income. And with the least experience and seniority, this age group is among the first to be laid off.

The 2008 and 2009 provisional birth data from the Centers for Disease Control and Prevention demonstrate what many women's service line leaders instinctively already knew: A decrease in births of 2% in 2008, and another big drop of 2.6% in 2009. This news was a relief for service line leaders who suspected they were the only ones behind budget.

In fact, in three years, the United States went from the highest number of births ever recorded (4,317,119 in 2007) to the lowest birth rate (13.5% in 2009) in at least a century.

Numerous studies indicate that stress decreases fertility. Amárach Research in Ireland, led by economist Gerard O'Neill, followed more than 18,000 births in 2009-2010 at two large maternity hospitals in Ireland and demonstrated a statistically significant relationship between low consumer confidence and decreased births nine months later. Data from The Pew Research Center published in April 2010 show a clear relationship between per capita income and the birth rate in 25 states: A decrease in per capita income almost exactly parallels a decreased birth rate (see Figure 4.1).

The falling prematurity rate was actually the first sign of the impact of the economy on the number of births. The childbearing demographic was already experiencing the recession in 2007. Births were impacted by early 2008. In its first quarter 2008 report, Pediatrix—the nation's largest publicly traded obstetrical and neonatal provider—reported its first-ever downturn, which Pediatrix attributed to fewer neonatal ICU (NICU) admissions.

FIGURE 4.1

BIRTH RATE TRACKS PER CAPITA INCOME—25 STATES

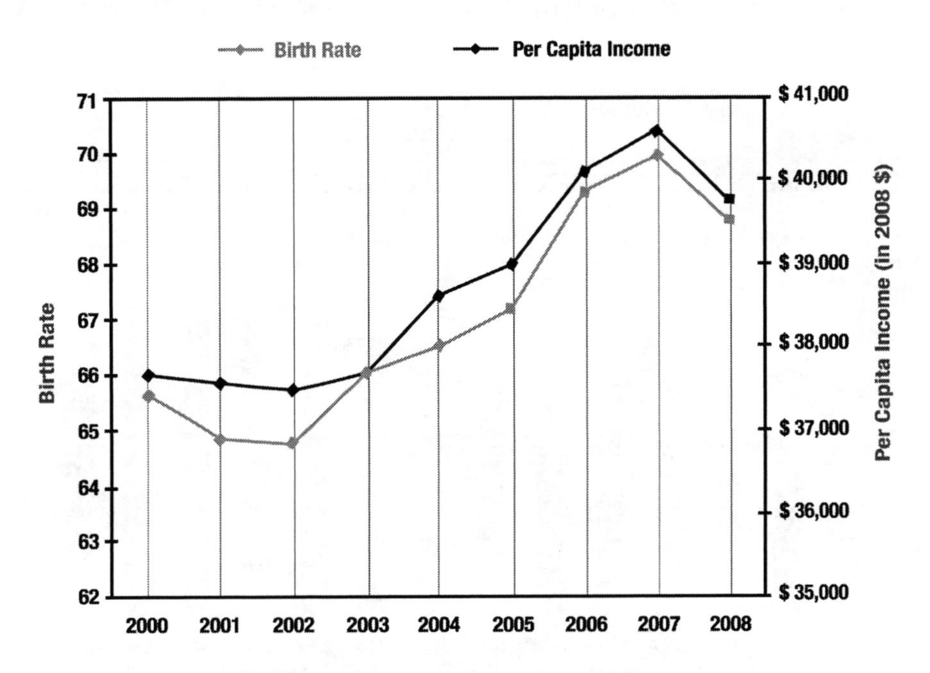

Note: Birth rate (general fertility rate) is the number of births per thousand women ages 15-44.

Sources: Statistics calculated using data from state government agencies, U.S. Census Bureau and Bureau of Economic Analysis

PewResearchCenter

Source: Pew Research Center, 2010, used with permission.

From 1990 through 2006, premature births increased more than 20%. Preliminary U.S. birth statistics now show that premature birth in 2007 took its first dip, a trend that was even stronger in 2008 and likely in 2009 (see Figure 4.2).

FIGURE 4.2

PRETERM BIRTH RATE AS PERCENT OF ALL BIRTHS, 1996–2008

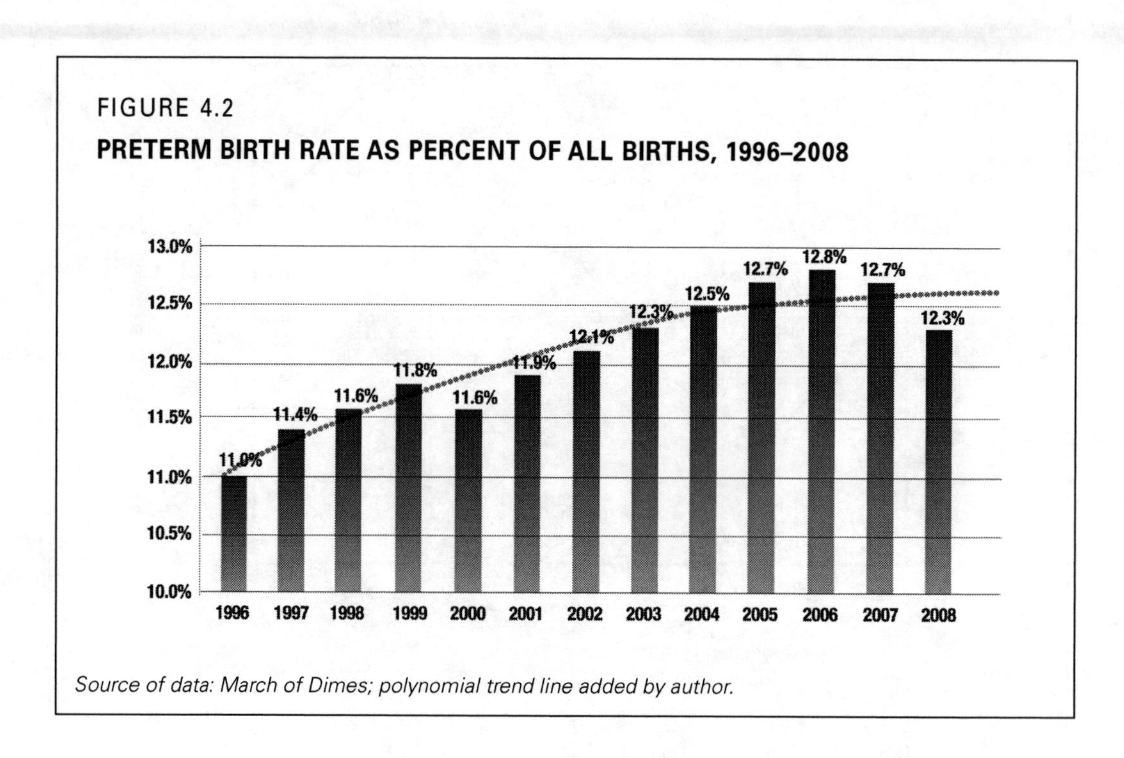

Source of data: March of Dimes; polynomial trend line added by author.

The decrease in neonatal admissions was fueled at least in part by a 2007 recession-related decrease in the assisted reproductive technology (ART) field. Other factors were also related to ART (i.e., embryo reductions), and an already-evident slowdown in other pregnancies. Most areas of the country have since seen a decrease in multiples (twins, triplets, and beyond) in the past three years. Commonly, ART results in multiples, which often are born prematurely. As a result, more than 60% of twins and 90% of triplets spend time in NICUs.

At the time, one in vitro fertilization cycle cost between $12,000 and $15,000 in the United States. With an average of three to four cycles required for pregnancy in this almost exclusively cash business, it becomes obvious why multiples appeared less in NICUs by early 2008. Cycle fees have decreased somewhat, and guarantees of pregnancy—with partial refunds if not achieved—have increased. But the economy and ethical issues stirred by such events as the birth of the California octuplets continue to hold down the multiples seen earlier in the decade.

During the late 1990s and early 2000s, larger families (four or more children) were a sign of affluence among well-off young parents. With a national swing to the political right during the same time frame, young religiously conservative-leaning families also were often larger.

The recession chilled both trends—two became enough for many.

Recently, there have been articles hinting that having an only child may become the nouveau chic among the affluent. During the Great Depression in the 1930s, about one out of five women did not bear children at all. Having one baby, or none, may or may not become a trend at this time, but the data do concern social economists who worry we might follow other developed countries with a below-replacement-rate level of births.

However, about 50% of pregnancies are unplanned, and even planned pregnancy can't be put off forever, particularly for the oldest Gen X women, now in their late 30s and early- to mid-40s. Both anecdotal evidence and early 2010 projections indicate women facing a biological time clock are deciding to take the risk. As the economy slowly returns, so will the babies.

The Pew report noted variances among the states in how the recession affected births, as did the Sg2 women's team, led by Rebecca Arbuckle, MBA, MHSA. Sg2 is a think tank combining advanced analytics, business intelligence, and education to the healthcare industry worldwide. Arbuckle says that some areas had increased births, others had decreased births, and some areas stayed the same. Many areas had decreased births in line with or greater than the national average—particularly those areas hit hard by the economic recession and lay-offs.

To create their projections, Sg2 studies baseline utilization, populations, epidemiology, economics and payment, systems of care, innovation and technology, and potentially avoidable admissions, then combines these impact factors to forecast trends in women's services.

Sg2 and others are also studying the impact of declining immigrant births, a trend seen in several 2008 national databases and it will likely show up in the 2009 data as well. Immigrants of any ethnicity tend to be younger, and therefore more likely to be childbearing. For example, the median age of non-Hispanic Caucasians in the United States is 38.1, compared with 26.5 for Hispanics.

Immigrants also tend to have larger families, and actual Hispanic growth in the United States over the next 20 years was projected in 2000 to be about double that of any other ethnicity—more than 1 million per year, as opposed to 500,000–600,000 per year for most other ethnicities. In addition, immigrants often work in jobs hit hard by the economy, such as construction and discretionary line items in household finances (e.g., contracted housekeeping and yard work). About 8% of U.S. births are to undocumented immigrants.

In 2000, there were 8 million undocumented immigrants in the United States. By 2007, that number peaked at about 12 million. The Department of Homeland Security says that it had decreased to 10.8 million by January 2009. A recent Pew Research Center report shows a similar drop.

The unexpected and significant decline in the U.S. birth rate in 2008 and 2009 has already brought economic comparisons to Japan's "lost decade" of economic decline in the '90s, when birth rates fell below population replacement rate.

The population replacement total fertility rate is about 2.1 children per woman. The United States has been slightly below that rate for the past decade at 2.0. Populations that maintain a total fertility rate of that low decline unless balanced by a large enough immigrant population to yield an overall population increase (births plus immigration) over deaths.

A decrease in the immigrant population, particularly given the huge coming influx of aging boomers, becomes a long-term socio-economic concern and will put a new twist on the political issue of immigration. Prior to the new birth data, U.S. immigration and birth trends were seen by economists as preventing the ultimate worry of a nation unable to take care of, and economically balance, its elderly population—a very real concern in countries like Japan. While the politics of this are one issue, the ramifications in women's services planning are less murky: When projecting care for women who will live longer than any generation before them, anticipate labor shortages, particularly for low-paying jobs in home and assisted care.

Other Sg2 projections for obstetrics include the following:

- Births will return to a 2%–3% annual growth rate over the next decade as the recession lessens.
- Cesarean deliveries will continue to increase in the short term, driven by advanced maternal age, greater co-morbidities, continued liability concerns, and cultural acceptance. Rates should level off around 40% in the latter part of this decade, in response to policymakers and payers.
- Inpatient obstetrics is primed for bundled payment. Physician payment is already a global fee, pregnancy and birth represent a high-volume discrete episode of care, and about 4 out of 10 births are already financed by the government (Medicaid).
- Get ready now for reimbursement to emerge for e-visits, both for routine OB and high risk. Once that happens, e-visits will really take off, with significant implications, particularly in high-risk detection, management, and outreach.
- Expect the case mix to continue to change upward toward more complexity.

Change is in the air

Hospitalists

The dramatic increase in use of OB/GYN hospitalists (sometimes referred to as laborists) in just a few years is only the beginning of change. For hospitals, laborists bring the potential of improved patient safety, patient flow, and safer management of high-risk walk-in cases. For young physicians, hospitalists promise the highly prized flexible lifestyle. Louis Weinstein, MD, in his depression-inducing reality check on "the unbearable unhappiness of the OB/GYN" says that hospitalists can relieve liability concerns and burnout among mature OB/GYNs.

Chris Swain, MD, an OB/GYN who, with his brother David, started OB Hospitalist Group, Inc., notes his group has a track record of improved patient safety and satisfaction, whether they deliver babies, staff OB triage, take care of walk-in unreferred patients, or are simply on site 24/7 to ensure immediate care in an emergency. An estimated 25% of all OB lawsuits are cases where a physician was not immediately available to deal with an emergency, so having the hospitalists on site 24/7 provides that backup. Unreferred call coverage alone does not improve the safety factor.

This U.S. modification of the European obstetrical care model may have taken a while to hit, but Gen X and Y physicians will glue some version of it in place. Overnight, a hospitalist program has become one of the top factors in recruiting new young physicians and even for medical students deciding whether to go into the OB/GYN specialty.

Information technology

Electronic health records (EHR) are being rapidly implemented, both in hospitals and physician offices, with the challenges that always accompany transformational change. We will all be better off once this is over, but in the meantime, watch out for many issues. Particularly beware of risk-increasing failure to develop order sets specific to obstetrics and neonatology. These services are already fraught with risk, and during EHR implementation, internal IT staff and vendors naturally focus on the 90% or so of integrated delivery system (IDS) business that is *not* high-risk obstetrics or neonatology. High-acuity pediatrics—increasingly centralized to very few hospitals—is in the same position.

The results can be hair-raising. Nationally, anecdotes from the trenches in academic centers to community hospitals range from head-scratching (the use of pounds as a weight measurement for 500-gram neonates) to terrifying (lack of specialty-specific order sets and emergency medications for major but infrequently occurring obstetrical and neonatal emergencies).

As you implement, make sure you talk with hospital and IDS specialty-specific peers who are already beyond implementation with your EHR vendor; get as high up as you can in the decision-making tree; link OB/GYN, maternal fetal medicine, and neonatology champions and IT gurus familiar with your highest-acuity needs at the start. Leverage your risk department when needed.

This process can take years and the average age of the implementers is often about 26 and they are attempting to work with a healthcare workforce with an average age in the 50s. The teachers are digital natives, the learners are digital immigrants, and the resultant digital communication gap alone is not insignificant. The increased risk that accompanies a lack of understanding of the unique issues in obstetrics or neonatology can be very expensive—in terms of lives, not just money.

CASE STUDY

Geisinger's Perinatal ProvenCare

As hospitals and providers race to implement EHRs, some early adopters are demonstrating how information technology and the IDS model can immensely impact both cost and quality.

One of these organizations is Geisinger Health System in Pennsylvania. Geisinger is an IDS with provider, facility, and health plan components—in other words, a great testing ground for the ACO concept. One of their most nationally-lauded initiatives is Geisinger ProvenCare.

The Perinatal ProvenCare initiative planning and implementation occurred during a 15-month period, and involved more than 4,000 pregnancies cared for in 22 clinics and performed in five hospitals (including three not owned by Geisinger). The initiative included more than 100 clinical and process improvement leaders.

This massive, multiple-site team reviewed—at the micro level—every process involved in care from before pregnancy to post-delivery, and redefined some 300 steps in care. The results of their Perinatal ProvenCare initiative are being published at about the same time as this book in several publications. But preliminary results include better outcomes for gestational diabetes mellitus, decreased premature rupture of membranes and a decreased AHRQ harm score at the same time as a dramatic decrease in both cesareans and NICU admissions.

Ruth Nolan, the vice president of operations for the women's health service line at Geisinger Health System, led the multidisciplinary, multi-team clinical effort. She says there is tremendous opportunity offered by the reach of the integrated delivery system and the infrastructure of EPIC, Geisinger's EHR. She notes, however, that not every entity involved was on EPIC at the time.

Currently, the U.S. infant mortality rate is 43 countries worse than the leader. We have always known that better prenatal care was the key to improving the neonatal and infant mortality rate, and Geisinger may be showing us just how to realize the benefits of prenatal care.

Growing body of knowledge: Evidence-based care

Signs are starting to emerge of a sharpened focus on whether what we do in obstetrics even makes sense. Remember that hospitalization for birth and the OB/GYN specialty are both less than a hundred years old; births occurred for millennia before women ever came to the hospital or dialed an obstetrician's office. The U.S. way of birthing is constantly evolving and not yet carved in stone by any means—particularly in an era when data about what actually works will be far more easily obtained with EHRs. Current obstetrical practices are increasingly being called into question.

The study, "The Cost of Being a Woman," by Kristen H. Kjerulff, et al., noted that U.S. annual total healthcare expenditure for female-specific conditions is estimated at $108 billion, with approximately one-third of these conditions being childbirth. Think of the description of the Geisinger Perinatal ProvenCare initiative and imagine the billions of dollars that could be saved nationally if obstetrical costs could be reduced.

The 2008 Milbank study on evidence-based maternity care—written for healthcare policy leaders—noted significant discrepancies between what the evidence says should be done in obstetrical care and what is actually being done. In March 2010, a consensus conference held by the National Institutes of Health (NIH) recommended that the American College of Obstetricians and Gynecologists (ACOG) reevaluate its guidelines for OB/GYNs on the issue of vaginal births after cesarean (VBAC).

ACOG issued somewhat less restrictive guidelines in July 2010 and the rumor is that more guidelines are being reviewed by ACOG. Nevertheless, what ACOG describes as an "onerous medical liability climate" will continue to drive professional recommendations.

Many variables are involved in creating or changing a cesarean rate that ranges nationally from the low teens—usually in hospitals with active nurse-midwifery programs—to more than 60%, with the preliminary 2008 average at 32.3%.

With the psychographic makeup of Gen X patients and physicians—combined with a litigious environment—it will be unclear for a while how much impact the new ACOG guidelines will have. However, once the government starts taking a stance, policy does usually change. The largest single barrier to significant change is probably the malpractice environment; tort reform could significantly impact decision-making and reduce costs. While Arbuckle notes there is some funding in the 2010 reform legislation for tort reform pilots, significant reform has so far been out of reach. If it were to occur, it would probably be after the 2012 elections.

Demographics

Socio-demographic changes and technological and scientific advances will continue to fuel the demand for ART, genetics, and maternal-fetal medicine (perinatology).

The average age of mothers at birth of a first child in the United States increased 3.6 years from 1970 to 2006, from 21.4 to 25.0. This phenomenon is not limited to the United States. In 2005, the average age of women at first birth was 29 in

Japan, 29+ in Germany, and 30 in New Zealand. The age of the mother at the first birth is an indicator about the overall age of pregnant women, fertility (and infertility), and the total number of births a woman will have. Those factors, in turn, affect the size, composition, and future growth of the population. Many sociocultural factors affect maternal age at first birth, from women's education and career options outside the home to the economy.

The aging of mothers is a key factor driving reproductive endocrinology and infertility (REI) service demand, which Sg2 predicts to grow 20% over the next decade, driven by age of mothers at first birth and improved technology and diagnostics. Sg2 notes that growth in this area is very market specific: Some areas are saturated, whereas there are still entire states without reproductive endocrinologists.

Increased maternal age also brings its own fertility, genetic, and obstetrical risks. Science and technology are keeping up, however. Technology always moves down the specialty chain, and most new improvements in obstetrical technology will continue to be introduced within perinatology first, and then adapted later by OB generalists.

Sg2's Arbuckle predicts increased demand for high-risk OB services, including significant increases in first trimester testing screening, medical management of pregnancy complications, and ultrasonography and other diagnostic techniques.

In addition to maternal age (and often linked to it), some of the factors driving increased utilization of perinatology include the growing prevalence of obesity and diabetes, growth in assisted reproduction technologies, new screening guidelines for fetal chromosomal abnormalities, as well as safer, less invasive procedures (see Figure 4.3).

FIGURE 4.3

EXPANDED COVERAGE AND HIGH-RISK PREGNANCIES WILL CAUSE RISE IN DEMAND

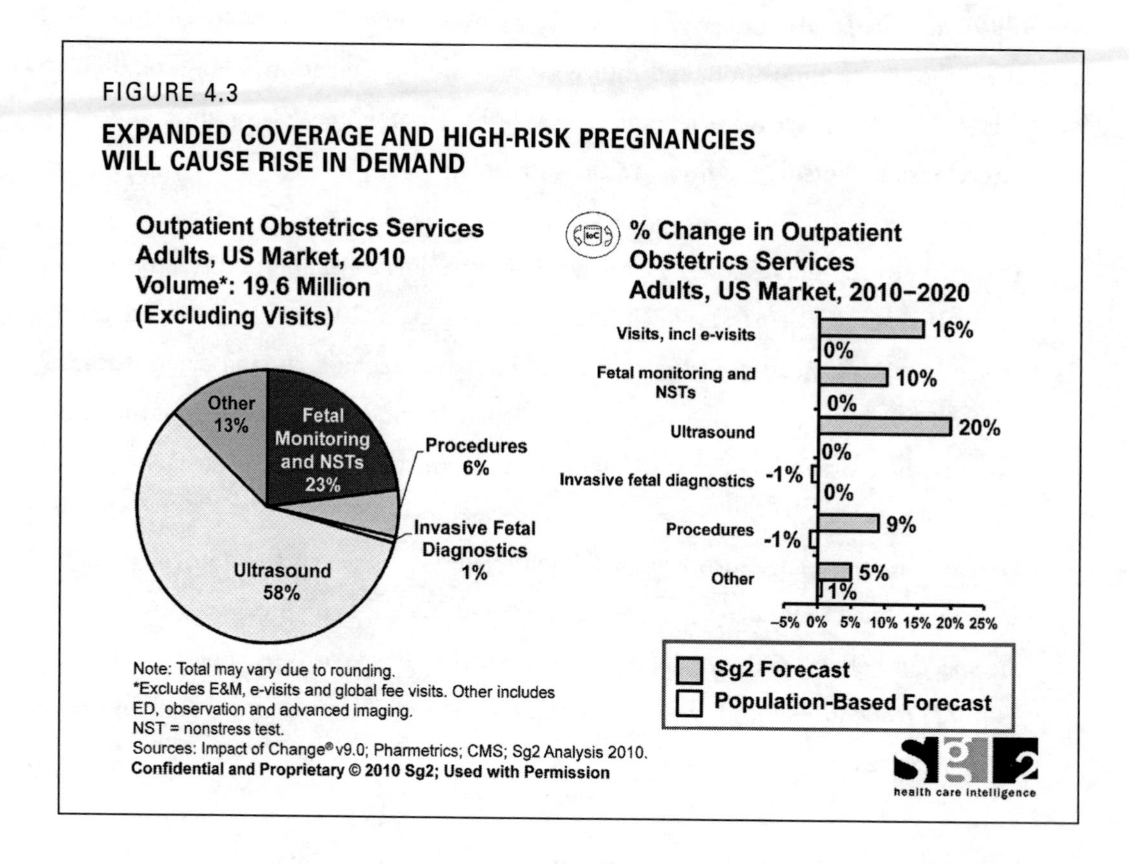

CASE STUDY

Perinatal care

As is the case with breast care, formalized comprehensive multidisciplinary perinatal care is coming of age. As part of its mission of improving healthcare for women and infants across the state, the University of North Carolina (UNC) has a long history with a coordinated multidisciplinary approach. Its Center for Maternal-Infant Health handles more than 500 cases of congenital defect statewide every year, with families referred from 10 minutes to three hours away, from private physicians, the military, and rural primary clinics.

Kathryn Menard, MPH, MD, maternal-fetal division director and vice chair for obstetrics at UNC, says the magic occurs at two places: the broadened level of learning among the multidisciplinary team members (neonatologists, perinatologists, geneticists, pediatric specialists, social workers, case managers, and nurses), and between providers and family.

The Center formally reorganizes the University's functional disciplinary infrastructure for these families, using case managers to navigate the family through prenatal care, labor and delivery, and NICU, and transitioning the family to long-term pediatric subspecialty care if needed. The case managers are the links among the various specialties, tying it all together for the family, arranging everything from transportation to provider teleconferences.

Nancy Chescheir, MD, professor and assistant dean for academic affairs for special projects, notes that the UNC approach focuses on the long-term health of the family, not just a procedure—from getting a military father back home in time for the birth to the complex social issues of a family dealing with fetal anomalies. The formalized team approach benefits remote providers and families as much as it does advanced learners at UNC, who otherwise work primarily within professional disciplines.

Telemedicine

Telemedicine shows exciting opportunities to leverage expertise over a far greater geographic area than in the past. The University of Arkansas ANGELS program was one of the first to expand statewide maternal-fetal outreach and access.

For an excellent example of integration of telehealth in traditional care in obstetrics—with decreased costs and vastly increased outreach—visit the ANGELS program website *(www.uams.edu/ANGELS)*. ANGELS has increased perinatal access, reduced complications of pregnancy, and saved millions of Medicaid dollars for the state. The program, which has a high patient satisfaction rating, has also cut NICU admissions.

Neonatology

Neonatology is downstream of reproductive technologies, maternal-fetal medicine, and routine pregnancies. Changes in practices in any of those three categories will change neonatal utilization.

With the introduction of the 39-week initiative limiting elective delivery below 39 weeks' gestation, many of us saw an immediate reduction in near-term admissions to special care units. However, acuity of the remaining census increased in relationship to total average daily census, keeping both sides of the neonatal admission/revenue equation balanced for the time being.

The 39-week initiative, however, may be only the first harbinger of the potential impact in NICU of evidence-based perinatal care. The Milbank report's list of "overused maternity interventions" includes everything from induction of labor to artificial rupture of membranes to continuous electronic fetal monitoring to epidural anesthesia—in short, just about everything that characterizes contemporary obstetrical practice.

Likewise, according to the report, evidence suggests that what we *don't* do—from more nurse midwifery-assisted birthing to non-supine positions for birth, VBACs, delayed cord clamping, and breast-feeding without any supplementation—is what we *should* be doing to improve pregnancy outcomes.

The Milbank report begs the question of what else might be causing iatrogenic NICU admissions. What else, if changed, might cause the very fast impact we saw on NICU admissions from the 39-week initiative? Improvements in perinatal diagnosis and treatment will likely balance the known risk factor of increasing age of the mother. The economy is expected to recover slowly, not as quickly as it plummeted.

For all these reasons, Sg2 predicts net zero growth in NICU (see Figure 4.4), which will likely force more centralized (IDS) and regionalized (state policy) neonatal care, at least for neonates requiring pediatric surgical teams.

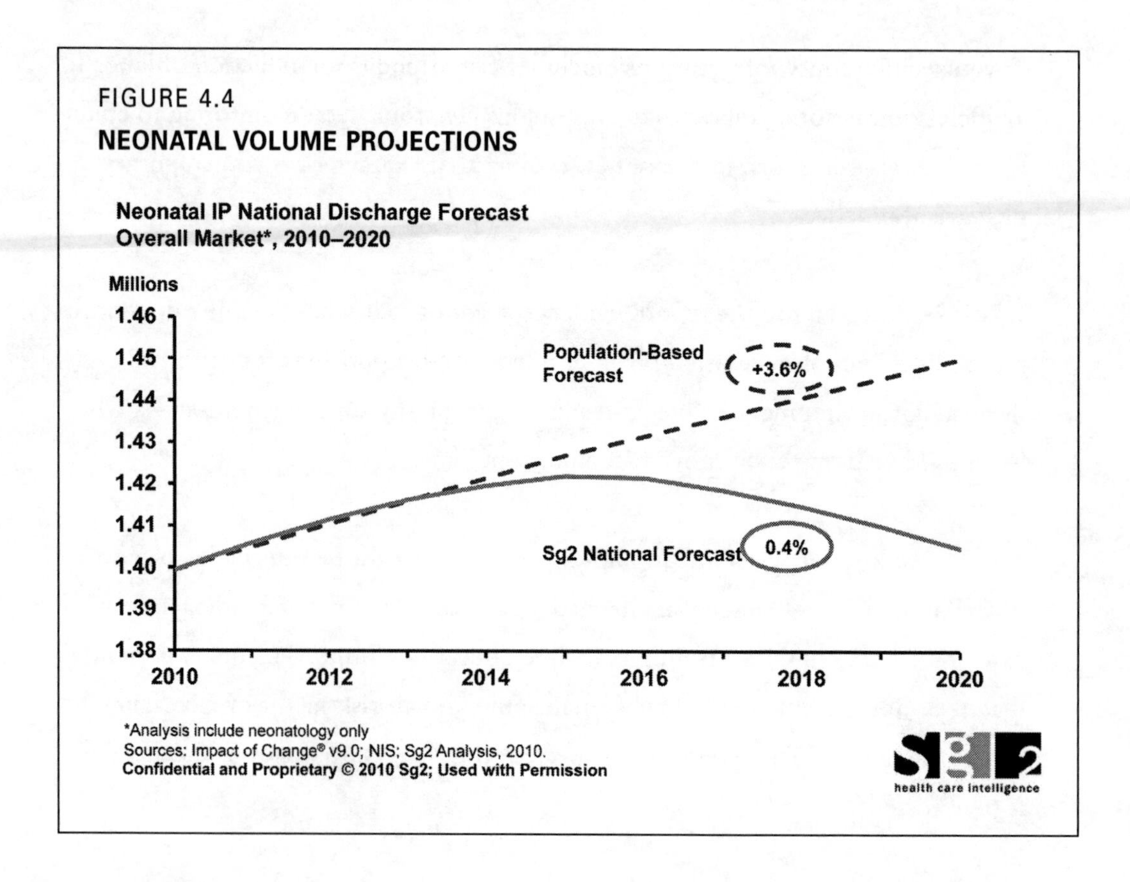

FIGURE 4.4
NEONATAL VOLUME PROJECTIONS

The aging of the baby boomer generation is a wild card that will play out in neonatology, in particular, over the next 20 years. Currently, as a nation, we spare few resources to save the lives of babies in neonatal intensive care units. Once boomers face the medical costs of aging, it's hard to imagine there will not be a clash over the allocation of resources. Combine boomer medical expectations with the power of AARP and escalating social security and Medicare costs, and the picture emerges. Sg2's Arbuckle notes there is already some budget-driven, state-specific pressure on appropriate level of care, coding, justification of length of stay, combined with some decreased reimbursement.

Non-Obstetrical Women's Services

Although the data are not as easily gathered as in obstetrics, many of the most significant changes in women's health will be in non-obstetrical services.

Gynecology

Three trends will accelerate changes in gynecology: subspecialization, greatly improved research and technology, and the movement to outpatient care.

Bolstered by a long-overdue national policy focus on medical research in women's health, advances in gynecology during the past decade have been monumental compared to prior years. Urogynecology and pelvic floor reconstructive surgery alone have gone from almost medieval to highly advanced approaches. There is much excitement in this area, which comes just in time for the demands of boomer women who aren't settling for weekly trips to the drug store for Depends. "Boomer women are not inclined to just live with it," says Rebecca Arbuckle at Sg2. "Boomers have more of a quest for quality of life in their later years than women in the past."

Almost all gynecological procedures have converted to the outpatient setting or have very short lengths of stay, and new procedures often only require minimally invasive surgery (MIS) techniques from the start. MIS has gained popularity as graduating residents have expanded MIS and robotic training. Robotic surgery is the great leveler. In the past, a lack of eye-hand coordination held back many surgeons from expanding into more MIS. Robotic surgery levels that playing field. Robotics is also in its infancy, but will likely follow the usual path of technology as innovative design yields more refinement in both devices and techniques and hopefully lowers capital investment costs.

Sg2 predicts significant declines in inpatient gynecology surgery in the next decade as care shifts to the outpatient environment (see Figure 4.5).

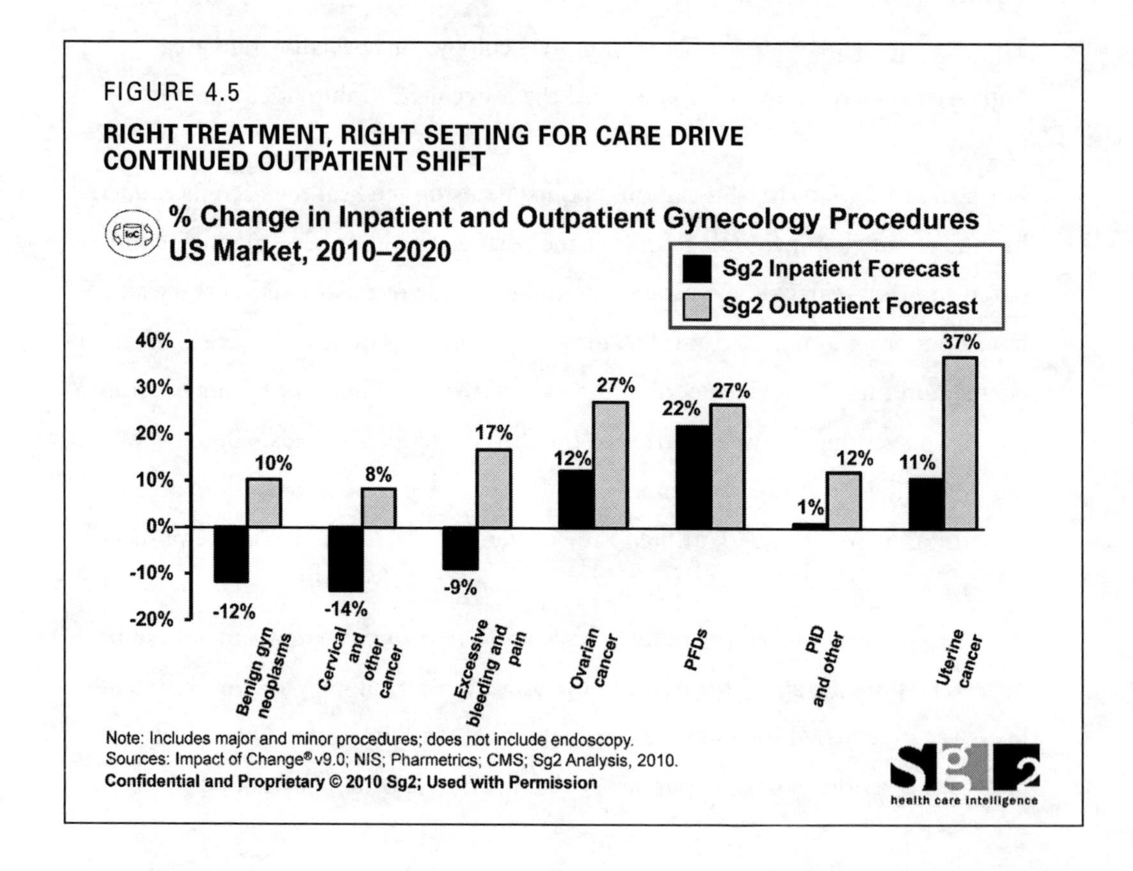

FIGURE 4.5

RIGHT TREATMENT, RIGHT SETTING FOR CARE DRIVE CONTINUED OUTPATIENT SHIFT

From Sg2's perspective, the most significant decline in non-malignant gynecology is in the area of benign gynecologic neoplasms, including fibroids and cysts, which represented just under one-third of 2009 gynecology admissions.

There are many reasons for the decline in admissions. There are an increasing number of alternatives to abdominal hysterectomy, from fibroidectomy to an increase in office-based procedures like endometrial ablation to uterine fibroid embolization. Boomer women, in particular, tend to be more interested in medical treatment or MIS rather than inpatient surgical options. In addition, women view bleeding and other benign issues as discretionary, so the current economy is reducing utilization as well.

Sg2 also predicts a decline in inpatient ovarian and cervical cancer admissions. Improved prevention—like the human papillomavirus vaccine—and advanced detection and treatment will change the picture of uterine and ovarian cancer over the long run, but in the short run, the literature is starting to support laparoscopic gynecologic oncology surgery. That will start the same type of sea change we saw in surgery for breast cancer, where almost all procedures done today are outpatient or very short inpatient stays.

While inpatient gynecology projections continue to decline, outpatient gynecology visits will increase, particularly as technology gets pushed down to the physician's office and Patient Protection and Affordable Care Act (PPACA) takes effect, improving access to providers, which will impact gynecology more than obstetrics. Kjerulff, et al, in their 2007 study, "The Cost of Being a Woman," found that uninsured women with "female-specific conditions" (e.g. obstetrics, gynecology) used healthcare much differently than their insured counterparts. Uninsured women visited a doctor less, filled prescriptions less, and were more likely to use the emergency room when these conditions became problematic. As healthcare access improves, the opposite could be inferred to occur, increasing provider utilization during a time of impeding physician shortages.

Potentially countering an increase in office gynecology visits are new recommendations on the frequency of routine exams. In late 2009, new clinical recommendations for the frequency of pap smears and mammography were published. While unfortunately presented from a public relations perspective, the news was still welcomed by many women, and the impact will be felt in the next few years. Arbuckle notes there may be a decrease in LEEP (loop electrosurgical excision procedure) and colposcopy as frequency of pap smears decreases. And, while we will not see a change in cervical cancer rates for quite a while, there will likely be less treatment of cervical precancer.

Fellowship-trained pelvic reconstructive surgeons are bringing a new level of sophistication beyond urogynecology alone, participating in complex multispecialty surgery with other gynecology, urology, colorectal, and related specialists. Pelvic floor disorders (PFD) now represent approximately 8% of inpatient gynecology admissions and 20% of outpatient gynecology. Over the next decade, Sg2 expects PFD inpatient admissions to grow by 22%, outpatient procedures and diagnostics to grow by more than 25%, and visits (including e-visits) to grow by 40%.

Breast

Nationally, breast care is quickly crossing discipline lines with comprehensive breast centers, pushed by the redefinition of multidisciplinary breast fellowships in the past five years, with the announcement of the first 15 comprehensive, multidisciplinary fellowship-training centers. Graduates are just now entering the job market and rewriting the approach to comprehensive breast care. The new fellowships focus on all aspects of breast care, not just cancer and not just surgery. Rotations are included with leading breast cancer risk assessment and management programs, breaking down barriers among the specialties and broadening the focus on true breast health, not just breast cancer.

The characteristics of IDS best practices in breast include a regional population–based approach, with centralized high-level diagnostics and care but decentralized screening. As with other disease entities experienced in great numbers by women, expect better research and resultant significant improvements in specificity, technology and whole-person, whole-life care.

PPACA mammography access will affect breast screening substantially, causing Sg2 to project much more utilization than population projections alone. New insurance plans are now required to cover the cost of preventive screening services like mammography, and Medicaid coverage expands in 2014. Between now and 2020, Sg2 predicts almost a 40% increase in screening mammography.

Everything else: Scalp to soles

In 2001, the Institute of Medicine (IOM) of the National Academy of Sciences officially announced that, at least for research purposes, women are different from men—you read that correctly: 2001. Before then, in medical research, the approach was enough to make even the most committed nonfeminist develop a headache.

In 1990, the General Accounting Office reported that for a variety of reasons, including concerns about pregnancy, women had been largely excluded from participation in medical research studies. As a result, four years later, the IOM called for more women to be included in clinical trials. In a separate 2001 report, the IOM noted "Historically, the research community assumed that beyond the reproductive system... differences [between men and women] do not exist or are not relevant."

The 2001 IOM report provided details that reportedly spurred the Society for Women's Health Research to successfully lobby Congress to include language in a 2005 appropriations bill that required the NIH to "include sex-based biology as an integral part" of research conducted by the 10 NIH institutes conducting a brain study. Without that requirement, the massive, incredibly expensive, groundbreaking multi-institute study apparently might not have included or differentiated women from men in 2005.

Many are now aware that, over the decades, much of cardiac research on the causes, detection, emergency, and ongoing treatment of heart attacks was based entirely on research on men. As a result, much of the knowledge available—and resultant teachings—apply poorly, or not at all, to women's heart disease—but without that research bias being known. As recently as 2005, researchers found that most cardiologists were still unaware of race and gender differences in the treatment of heart disease.

One of my personal favorites has always been the listing of "typical" heart attack symptoms—those that men have. On that particular slide, the other column is always "atypical"—the signs women often experience.

Unfortunately for all of us, the concept of men as "typical" and women as "atypical" has dominated medical research until recently. Those researchers involved in gender-based medical care all say the same thing: When providers start learning about and applying gender-based care principles for women, gender-based care for men improves as well because of the heightened awareness.

The IOM also says that "gender-based" labels confuse the issue, and that "sex-based" is more appropriate. The term "sex" is genetically determined by a person's reproductive organs and chromosomes, whereas "gender" refers to a person's self-representation as male or female. This is a solid scientific differentiation, although the term "gender-based" still is more prevalent in much of the literature when referring to sex-differentiated studies or programs.

The IOM report then went on to talk about very basic gaps in knowledge. "While it is anatomically obvious why only males develop prostate cancer and only females get ovarian cancer, it is not at all obvious why, for example, females are more likely than males to recover language ability after suffering a left-hemisphere stroke or why females have a far greater risk than males of developing life-threatening ventricular arrhythmias in response to a variety of potassium channel-blocking drugs."

The IOM identified two key issues caused by the lack of sex differentiation in research:

- The need to conduct more research on the role of sex
- The critical importance of changing the practices of physicians (approximately 750,000 in the United States alone) who, even today, unknowingly base diagnosis and treatment on results biased by the exclusion of women or by sex-undifferentiated research findings

And millions of physician from other countries have been trained in the U.S. or influenced by U.S. medical research; the implications are world-wide.

The 2001 report generated 14 recommendations, some as basic as "study sex differences from womb to tomb." As Mary-Lou Purdue, PhD, from the IOM notes, "Sex does matter. It matters in ways that we did not expect. Undoubtedly, it also matters in ways we have not begun to imagine."

Unleashed by the 2001 report, the literature is now replete with examples of the pervasive influence of male-only research. The best summary—sobering at best—is probably found on the website of the Office of Women's Health (U.S. Department of Health and Human Services), which summarizes multiple studies. One example is from a 2000 study (Nicolette and Jacobs), which included studies of coursework in medical schools:

> *In our analysis ... we found that four out of the five cases described male patients. This is consistent with traditional male imagery in medical education, including textbook and lecture illustrations, as well as case examples. Discussions involving female patients have traditionally been relegated to*

reproductive health, mental illness, and pregnancy-related illness. This may affect trainees of medicine in two ways: encouraging the misperception of men's health as the 'norm' in medicine with women's health as a deviation from this standard, and contributing to the designation of a disproportionate number of female patients' complaints to mental, rather than systemic, illness.

OPPORTUNITIES TO IMPROVE WOMEN'S HEALTH

- Teach gender- and evidence-based medicine
- Develop larger multidisciplinary, higher acuity women's program development, leveraging new fellowship-trained subspecialists
- Implement EHR-generated data capabilities for women's research in areas beyond obstetrics and gynecology
- Obtain gender-specific research grants to prove outcomes
- Launch niche programs in women's healthcare
- Research how to integrate complementary and alternative medicine (CAM) in mainstream programs
- Study the processes of death and dying, with changes in palliative care and home care, including a return to in-home care and even home hospitalists
- Add gerontologists, palliative care, and other providers for aging and chronic illness
- Add rehabilitation specialists of every type, from pelvic floor to stroke to flexibility and balance.

There is much to do, and now, with increased awareness and policy boosts, much opportunity. New program frontiers in women's health abound, as do research possibilities. For generations, women have known—or at least suspected—that the medical research and recommended treatments often didn't always make sense. Boomer women are often particularly cynical given their life experiences, from high-dose oral contraceptives in the 1960s to the déjà vu hormone replacement therapy/estrogen experience of this decade.

For instance, there are at least 40 easily identifiable conditions that women experience more or differently than men from adolescence to aging, ranging from behavioral to colorectal, to renal and lung disease, and even to trauma and ICU outcomes. Opportunities abound for niche programs in women's health by leveraging your strengths in areas outside reproductive health. In many areas, these differences are still unrecognized—even in heart disease. With willing providers and by educating women, you have the ability to make an immediate difference in morbidity and mortality, with new research showing up almost daily.

Rebecca Arbuckle puts it well: "We have come to the point that we acknowledge that women are different. We are starting to understand the why/how. The future of female-focused care will be a comprehensive understanding and agreement of how female biology and physiology impacts the care pathway, answering the question, "what do we do about it."

Complementary and alternative medicine

Another trend that just won't go away, despite years of indifference among practitioners of Western medicine, is that of complementary and alternative medicine (CAM). In particular, the persistence of the bioidentical hormone debate since the 1930s has become a classic case study.

Boomer women, who first brought Lamaze to the United States in the '60s, have a long history of being cynical about the authority of mainstream medicine and have never stopped their tradition of looking for answers elsewhere. Boomer women, in particular, have refused to buy in to the cautions of Western medicine about alternatives. They will continue to explore Eastern and other alternatives, particularly as they develop chronic diseases. The Internet facilitates that search in both good and bad ways: Great alternative sites are easily available, from the NIH CAM site to Dr. Andrew Weil to the Harvard-developed Benson-Henry Institute for Mind Body Medicine to advice from board-certified, well-credentialed physicians and pharmacologists. But there are also recommendations with no history, testing, or basis for use other than hope or personal passion.

Other hot topics in CAM right now include:

- Non-pharmacologic management techniques for cardiovascular disease (think meditation, yoga, and even 70% cocoa dark chocolate, among others)
- The well-documented positive impact of guided imagery, tai chi, healing touch, and energy therapies, among others
- Herbal and food supplements, particularly accessed by women
- Stress reduction
- Probiotic use

- Metabolic syndrome, hormones, and weight management
- Thyroid and adrenal fatigue

Finally, link the heightened debate over the use of medical marijuana not to younger generations, but to boomers, who came of age in the '60s and are now developing chronic illnesses and facing limited resources postretirement. This is just one of the ways boomers will rewrite chronic illness, aging, and even death. Just as they rewrote birthing, boomer women will do the same with death and dying—bringing a holistic reality orientation and compassion back into the process.

The new seniors

Seniors and leading-edge boomer women still have a lot of loyalty. If you don't have a senior program, now is a great time to develop one as leading-edge boomers move into retirement age.

In addition to the psychographics of boomers already discussed, boomers are engaged in a battle against the concept of getting old. Most of them reject anything labeled "50 plus," let alone being 60, and they won't accept 70 or 80 any more easily. For better or worse, expect much more preoccupation with not looking or feeling old—skin, hair, general body, and supplements. That may even include cosmetic gynecology, which already has firm roots in Florida, Las Vegas, California, and New York. Less pricey treatments that mitigate the bodily impact of aging will continue to develop, with escalating demand. The ads might not mention aging, but the message will be received.

Boomers are already rewriting rehabilitation after previously "just live with it" conditions like stroke and joint surgery. The need for rehabilitation will increase dramatically, as will low-impact community exercise programs that assist balance and flexibility, increase bone density, and provide a post-retirement social network.

Summary

For obstetrics and neonatology, here are the highlights:

- The babies will return, slowly but surely; you can't put off having a baby forever.

- The winds of change are in the air for obstetrical practices, indicating that some public policy limits may have been reached on issues like the escalating cesarean rates.

- Changes are also on the horizon in neonatology, with fluctuating census already affected negatively by the economy and the 39-week initiative. Worldwide improved prenatal care has always been related to fewer NICU admissions. As evidence-based OB care and better fetal diagnostics kick in, NICU admission rates will likely remain flat despite increased maternal risk factors.

- Generational expectations of Gen X and Gen Y physicians and patients will continue to change the face of obstetrical practices in such areas as the use of OB/GYN hospitalists/laborists.

- Technology, demographics, and psychographics will continue to push the need for reproductive endocrinology and maternal-fetal medicine.

- Telemedicine shows great promise to decrease costs and inexpensively expand outreach, leveraging maternal-fetal expertise in particular.

- Should it ever occur, tort reform could have a huge impact on the outcomes of birth in the United States and world, as the influence of U.S. medical education is worldwide.

The following are some highlights in overall women's care:

- Implementation of EHRs is causing the expected transformational disruption on many fronts and can increase risk in obstetrics and neonatology if not carefully implemented. However, the promise of EHR is significant, and there is early, exciting evidence that it will facilitate true evidence-based medicine.

- PPACA will increase OB/GYN utilization on several fronts, from improved access to prenatal care—hopefully reducing risk—granting new access to screening and prevention, and increasing physician and outpatient utilization. However, the impact will be seen far more in office and outpatient care, not inpatient services.

- Telehealth is on the verge of practicality, and can dramatically and quickly influence access and outcomes.

- Gynecology is headed firmly down a path of subspecialization, minimally invasive procedures, and outpatient (versus inpatient) stays.
- While women's health has historically been significantly under-researched, the nascent identification of sex-/gender-related health issues promises niche opportunities to quickly influence women's health clinical and business development.
- Research opportunities for sex-based solutions have opened up immensely in the last decade. Now the challenge is to integrate them into daily practice at all levels of healthcare—for the benefit of both men and women.
- Boomers will force significant change in every aspect of aging, death, and dying—just as they did with birthing and delivery.
- Changes brought by boomers will depend not just on mainstream medicine, but on integration of East and West, leveraging CAM to support and enhance mainstream care.
- There will be a shortage of providers and programs in palliative care, rehabilitation, and hospice and home care, with a significant shift, again, to out-of-hospital care.

And, finally, in all aspects of women's health, regardless of any particular clinical or business development focus, Arbuckle of Sg2 notes we have progressed from "build it and they will come" through "buy it and they will come" to the era now of "prove it and they will come" (see Figure 4.6.). This presents both an exciting and a daunting challenge, one where women's service line executives have a huge opportunity to lead the entire organization.

FIGURE 4.6
WOMEN'S HEALTH MUST CONTINUE TO PROVE PERFORMANCE

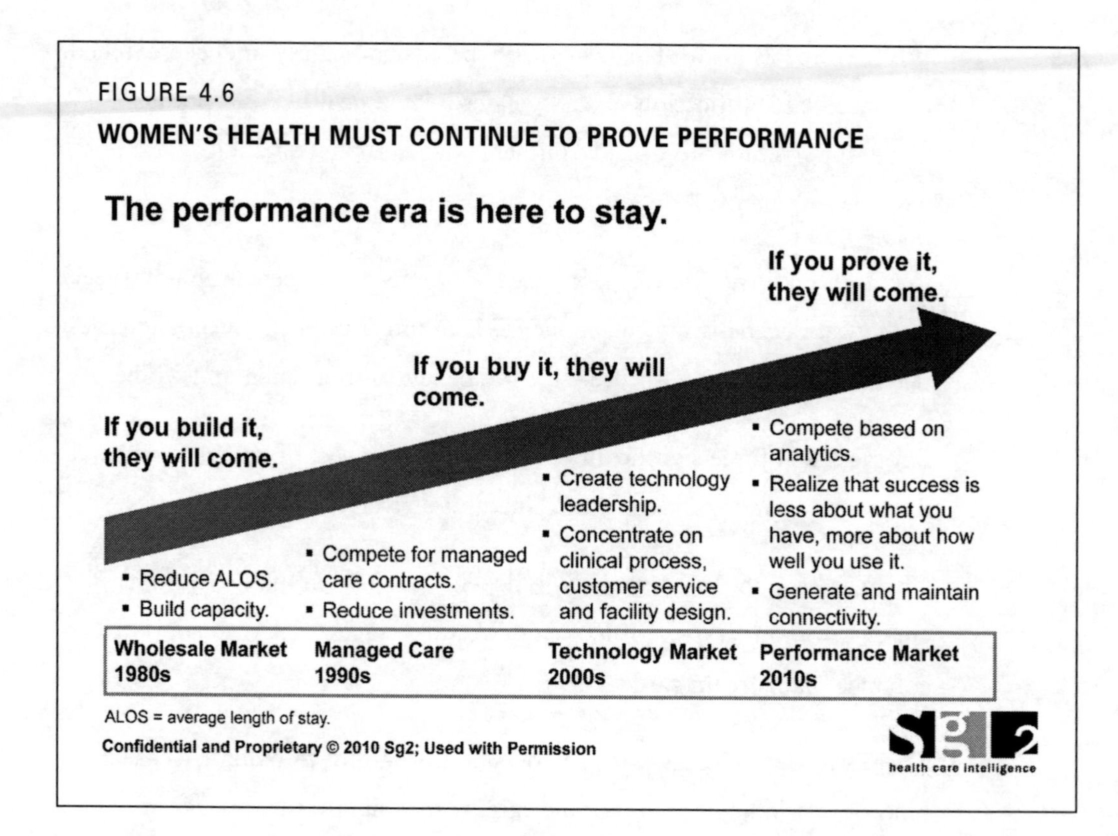

References

Agency for Healthcare Research and Quality, U.S. Department of Health and Human Services. "Overview of Hospitals and Hospital Procedures in the United States." 2003. *www.ahrq.gov/data/hcup/factbk7/factbk7b.htm*

American Association of Colleges of Nursing. Nursing Shortage Fact Sheet, 2010.

American College of Obstetricians and Gynecologists. "OB-Gyns Issue Less Restrictive VBAC Guidelines." July 21, 2010. *www.acog.org/from_home/publications/press_releases/nr07-21-10-1.cfm.*

Centers for Disease Control and Prevention. "Births, Marriages, Divorces, and Deaths: Provisional Data for 2009." *National Vital Statistics Report* 58(25).

DeFrances, Carol, Lucas, Christine, Buie, Verita, and Golosinskiy, Aleksandr. "2006 National Hospital Discharge Survey." Centers for Disease Control and Prevention's Division of Health Care Statistics. July 2008. *www.cdc.gov/nchs/data/nhsr/nhsr005.pdf*

Fears, Daryl. "Retirements by Baby-Boomer Doctors, Nurses Could Strain Overhaul." *The Washington Post* (June 14, 2010). *www.washingtonpost.com/wp-dyn/content/article/2010/06/13/AR2010061304096.html.*

Healthcare Cost and Utilization Project Facts and Figures. "Statistics on Hospital-Based Care in the United States." 2006. *www.hcup-us.ahrq.gov/reports/factsandfigures/facts_figures_2006.jsp#ex3_1*

Hoefer, Michael, Rytina, Nancy, and Baker, Bryan C., U.S. Dept. of Homeland Security. "Estimates of the Unauthorized Immigrant Population Residing in the United States: January 2009." Population Estimates (January 2010). *www.dhs.gov/xlibrary/assets/statistics/publications/ois_ill_pe_2009.pdf.*

Institute of Medicine, National Academy of Sciences. "Exploring the Biological Contributions to Human Health: Does Sex Matter?" 2001. *www.iom.edu/~/media/Files/Report%20Files/2003/Exploring-the-Biological-Contributions-to-Human-Health-Does-Sex-Matter/DoesSexMatter8pager.pdf.*

Kjerulff, Kristen H., Frick, Kevin D., Rhoades, Jeffrey A., and Hollenbeak, Christopher S. "The Cost of Being a Woman: A National Study of Health Care Utilization and Expenditures for Female-Specific Conditions." *Women's Health Issues* 17 (2007): 13–21.

Livingston, Gretchen, and Cohn, D'Vera, Pew Research Center. "U.S. Birth Rate Decline Linked to Recession." Pew Research Center Publications (April 6, 2010). *http://pewresearch.org/pubs/1552/birth-rates-united-states-decline-recession.*

Lowery, Curtis, et al. "ANGELS and University of Arkansas for Medical Sciences Paradigm for Distant Obstetrical Care Delivery." *American Journal of Obstetrics & Gynecology* 196 (June 2007): 534.e1–9.

March of Dimes, 2010. *www.marchofdimes.com/peristats.*

Medical Group Management Association annual surveys, 2007 through 2009 (data years 2006 through 2008), Colorado.

National Center for Complementary and Alternative Medicine, part of the National Institutes of Health: *http://nccam.nih.gov.*

National Institutes of Health. "Final Panel Statement." NIH Consensus Development Conference on Vaginal Birth After Cesarean: New Insights (March 2010). *http://consensus.nih.gov/2010/vbacstatement.htm.*

OB Hospitalist Group, Inc. *www.obgynhospitalistgroup.com.*

Organisation for Economic Co-operation and Development (OECD). "Mean Age of Mother at First Birth." OECD Family Database, updated January 2010. *www.oecd.org/dataoecd/62/49/41919586.pdf.*

Passel, Jeffrey S., and Cohn, D'Vera, Pew Research Center. "U.S. Unauthorized Immigration Flows Are Down Sharply Since Mid-Decade." Pew Research Center Publications (September 2010). *http://pewresearch.org/pubs/1714/annual-inflow-unauthorized-immigrants-united-states-decline.*

Sakala, Carol, and Corry, Maureen P. "Evidence-Based Maternity Care: What It Is and What It Can Achieve." Milbank Report (2008). *www.milbank.org/reports/0809MaternityCare/0809MaternityCare.html.*

Schneider, Mary Ellen. "Laborist Programs Manage OB Triage." *OB-Gyn News* 44(9) (July 2009).

Uncommon Insights, LLC. "Literature Review on Effective Sex- and Gender-Based Systems/Models of Care." The Office on Women's Health (2007). *www.womenshealth.gov/owh/multidisciplinary/reports/GenderBasedMedicine/Question6.cfm.*

Weinstein, Louis. "The Unbearable Unhappiness of the Ob-Gyn: A Crisis Looms." *OBG Management* 20(12) (December 2008).

CHAPTER 5

Laying the Foundation

With the external healthcare environment and women's health trends providing a foundation, it's time to take a look at some of the internal variables that will shape how you develop or strengthen your women's health service line. The visioning process for your service line takes place long before you hold a retreat. First, you need to use the knowledge you have about the external and internal environment to develop your own vision of where you'd like to see your organization, your service line, and you—personally and professionally.

Visioning and Planning for Success

There are five basic steps in any successful project. You may think of these steps as a guide for short projects, but it's just as useful for something complex, such as starting a service line or stepping up a service line's capabilities as the organization grows and matures. Viewing something complex within the same project management structure can help you get your arms around the tasks and the people needed to carry it through to completion. You can see the beginning, interim goals, and end—and it's easier to normalize reactions when put in context of the entire project.

Whether you're starting a service line, envisioning the future in an existing service line, or simply starting a new program, the same five steps apply: visioning, planning, action, shaping or momentum, and stabilization (see Figure 5.1). Successful projects always follow and, importantly, complete this cycle.

FIGURE 5.1

STAGES OF SUCCESSFUL PROJECTS

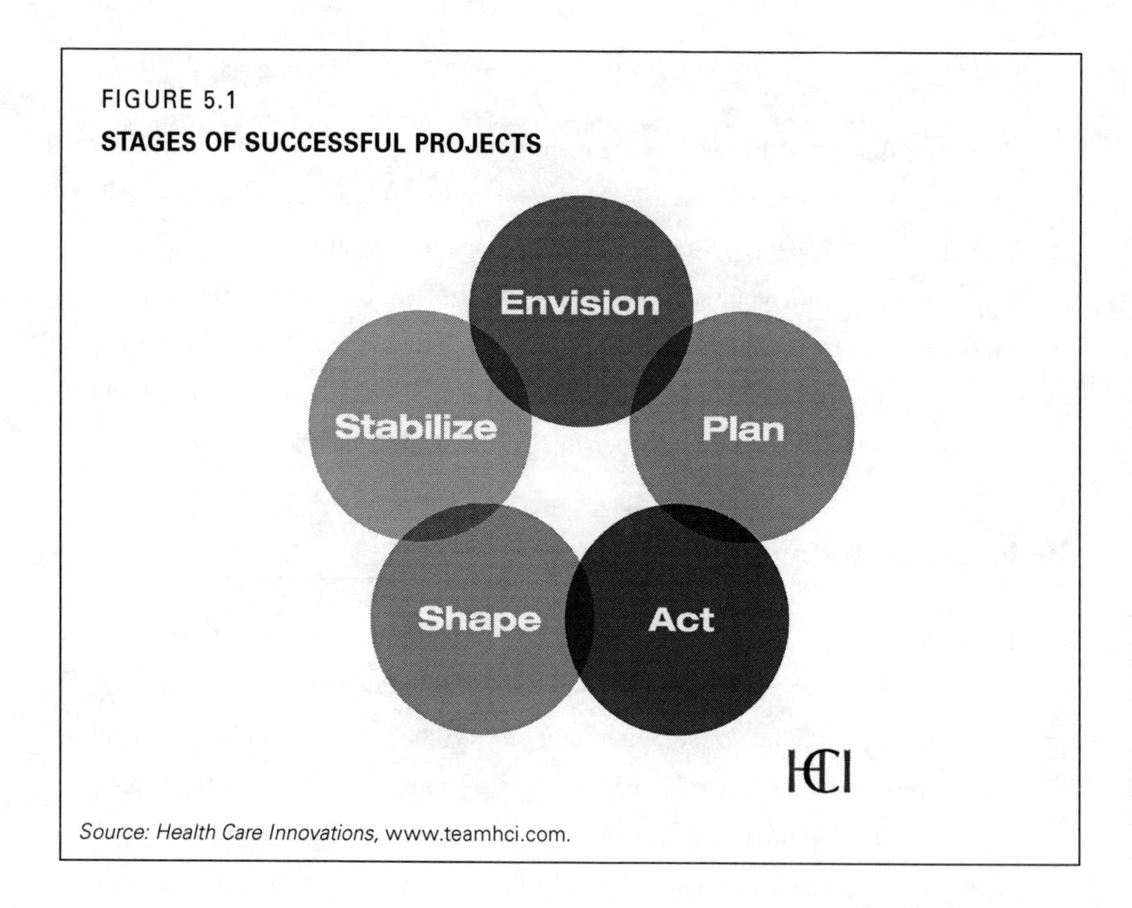

Source: Health Care Innovations, www.teamhci.com.

The internal landscape

One of the most interesting aspects of the phases of a successful project is that all of us inherently relate more to one phase of the cycle than the others—sort of a home phase, an intuitive comfort zone. As we mature, we get more comfortable with the phases on either side as well, even the ones we like least; we understand and value them more than we do earlier in our careers and trust others to help us in areas where we do not have an intuitive comfort zone. Regardless, our home phase is where we are most comfortable, and we will revert there when the opportunity arises, so awareness is key to long-term success.

Building a complete team

With physicians and nurses, it's pretty easy to figure out their home phase just by looking at their preferred clinical position. Consider the clinical area you ended up in—your specialty or focus. If it's in a high-acuity area, like labor and delivery, ICU, neonatal ICU (NICU), emergency department (ED), or surgery, you're most comfortable with the "act" part of this cycle. If it's in postpartum, newborn nursery, or medical-surgical floors, you're most comfortable in the "shape," "stabilize" or sometimes "plan" portion of the cycle.

There's a reason cross-training in OB is difficult to accomplish; this intuitive comfort zone is why. Providers like nurse-midwives who enjoy all phases—prenatal care through delivery through postdelivery and lactation—are unusual, not the norm. The disdain that can occur between the "act" and the "stabilize" groups alone has never failed to amaze me throughout my career. Effective healthcare needs both groups. In a true emergency, the event doesn't call for someone doing visioning or thoughtfully thinking through a plan. On the other hand, mothers would fail at their core identity—successfully mothering a child—without maternal-infant/postpartum and newborn nurses and lactation consultants who teach mothers how to survive and thrive beyond birth.

The whole process of thinking through these phases is the same reason to know your Myers-Briggs® or Personalysis type. It's about you, but it's also about your collaborative relationships with others who are not like you—a critical professional maturation point. It's about building a complete team—using a whole brain, not half a brain. Naturally, we are attracted to people like us. But you should ensure that you have a well-rounded team with varying personalities, or components of your service line may suffer.

Service line leaders need to answer the following questions:

- Who is doing the visioning? Not just an idea for tomorrow or this year, but a true vision of the future—something that doesn't yet exist.
- Who are your planners and where are they? Who can apply business and finance analysis to the vision and test it?
- What is your own tendency? Do you get stuck in planning and seem unable to get a project off the ground, or do you act quickly when asked a question and attack the problem right away, often surprised at pushback?
- If you are an "act" person, who takes over the project and runs with it when you move on to something else?

- Who will stabilize the new project and make sure it doesn't need to be re-invented every day for lack of consistent application? Who will orient newcomers to the culture and goals? Who writes the stabilization documents, such as policies and procedures? Who stabilizes the new program so it can be marketed?

For example, people who love the "act" phases tend to enjoy kicking off projects, but not actually getting the project done. The critical testing and tweaking inherent in the "shape" stage may seem boring to this group. On the other hand, if you're an "act" person, you won't get bogged down in a protracted planning phase—you will know when it's time to get going. However, you may want to contract out visioning and find someone to pick up the "shape" components of the project when you get tired of it. In addition, you will need someone who excels in the "stabilize" stage to make sure the desired outcomes are embedded into policies so the project sticks around longer than one or two months.

Every type has a story about the other of personalities. Planners often view the "act" phase as premature, or unnecessary chaos. Planners may have difficulty letting go of the planning phase when the project needs to get going. Shapers and stabilizers also can see the "act" phase as unnecessarily disruptive.

Organizations tend to reflect these leadership styles. High "act" organizations—those built around action—often never stabilize. Every day brings a new emergency, which further feeds the hunger for action. One of my favorite examples of this is a new hospital that, for several years, never named or developed directional signing for its much-used conference rooms. That meant someone had to jump up and accompany anyone who needed to get to one of the conference rooms, leaving his or her own work station unmanned.

Likewise, there are hospitals that are ultra-stabilized, where change occurs against organizational resistance at every turn, and cognitive dissonance is the reaction to even the simplest suggestion of change. Accomplishing change in these organizations takes a huge amount of commitment and perseverance—and a lot of personal and professional support.

Before you get started building or expanding your women's health service line, take the time to evaluate your team and your organization. Make sure you know your team and resources—who can help you with visioning, who are the planners, who is the action person, who picks up that ball and runs with it, and who stabilizes all of it so it becomes second nature and is supported by culture, staff members, policies, and procedures.

Systemness and service line development

Determining where your organization is in system development is essential because that developmental stage will drive service line development as well. Figure 5.2 provides general stages of development that you can use to determine where you are in the women's service line development map.

FIGURE 5.2

STAGES OF SERVICE LINE DEVELOPMENT

	Healthcare organization	Women's service line focus	Women's service line leadership
1980s	• Hospital	• OB primarily • Minor gynecology • Diagnosis-related group bundling/ financial analysis	• OB/GYN "super manager" with an operations focus
1990s	• Hospital, start of integrated delivery systems (IDS)	• More gynecology with growth of subspecialties • Women as key for family patient acquisition	• Marketing executive
2000s	• IDS consolidation (and parallel play)	• OB/GYN and early gender medicine • System strategy	• Business development skills
2010s	• Further consolidation • Accountable care organizations?	• Greater scope • Gender-based care • Women as key to decrease unnecessary utilization in family	• Physician leadership roles; dyads

These general stages are organized by decade, but specific organizations and regions may have reached a particular stage earlier or later. The way you proceed will vary depending on whether you are starting a service line or maturing it, whether you are in an independent hospital or an integrated delivery system (IDS), and whether your service line role is primarily business development, marketing, or operations.

The organizational structure of the service line depends completely on the scope of responsibility and outcomes expected by the organization.

Accountabilities

One of the most frequently asked questions I hear is what portion of operations responsibility service line leaders should have, if any.

The answer depends on the situation. The following are some significant variables:

- Whether the service line is arranged around a disease process or condition (heart, orthopedics), around populations (like women's service line), or around technology or a treatment process (surgery, ED)
- Whether the service is for one hospital, two or more, or whether it is for an IDS
- And finally, specific to women's health, whether you have an OB/GYN service line or a women's service line—a very important distinction

The justification for service line goes back to positioning the health system and achieving that position. Operations and service line both play critical roles in ensuring that the organization grows and thrives (see Figure 5.3). However, the focus of each is different.

FIGURE 5.3

ORGANIZATIONAL FOCUS

Operations	Service line
Focus: Process	Focus: Outcomes
Functional departments	Interdisciplinary
Authoritative clinical and product knowledge	Market-driven curiosity about the unmet needs, issues of customers and consumers
Manage value	Create and balance value

Another way to look at the differences is to focus on complementary roles between operations and service line management (see Figure 5.4).

FIGURE 5.4

COMPLEMENTARY ROLES: OPERATIONS AND SERVICE LINE

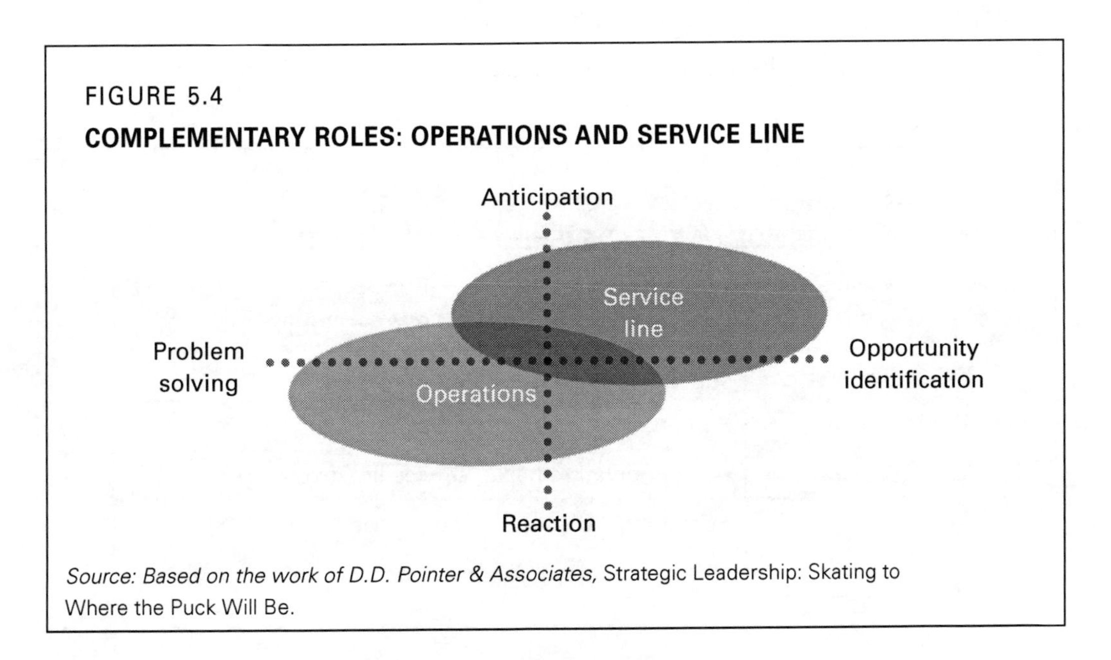

Source: Based on the work of D.D. Pointer & Associates, Strategic Leadership: Skating to Where the Puck Will Be.

Strategy is the justification for establishing service lines. Within an IDS service line, operations become secondary to achieving that goal. Historically, the "super manager" service line leader—who is focused primarily on operations, not strategy—is often one of the first to be laid off during periodic hospital cost-cutting. When the primary focus is operations, it's difficult to focus on strategy because too much is happening daily in operations alone.

In a strategy-focused service line position, how the mix of operations and strategy plays out depends on the setting. In a single hospital, for instance, there may not be justification for a full-time position dedicated to strategy and positioning, and that role may naturally fall to an already-existing excellent operations leader in women's health. By the time you get to IDS, particularly in a population-based service line like women's health, operational oversight has to play second fiddle to strategy. But there are always variations. In a women's hospital, strategy often takes place within operations with business development performing R&D, for example.

FIGURE 5.5

EXAMPLES OF SERVICE LINE LEADERSHIP ACCOUNTABILITY

Scope	Service line operations accountability?
Single hospital	Often
Two hospitals	Sometimes
IDS	Rare: Population-based service line (women's)
	Sometimes: Disease-based service line (OB/GYN)
	Often: Technology/Treatment-based service line (ED)

If present at the IDS level, operational responsibility is usually in a single clinical area that is critical to the organization for bottom-line results, or that needs the direct, temporary hand of the service line leader to achieve significant change.

Women's or an OB/GYN service line?

In many organizations, a women's health service line started as an OB/GYN service line, which is a disease-based service line like orthopedics or cardiovascular. In OB/GYN service lines, the service often does include operational responsibility for obstetrics, newborn and/or neonatology, and gynecology, and sometimes breast. Historically, the OB/GYN service line was hospital-centric, arising at a time when gynecology was still primarily inpatient-focused. There is a rationale for that; obstetrics and gynecology comprise an important part of the business of many hospitals and systems, even though most gynecology services are moving quickly to outpatient settings.

In the 1990s, the hospital-centric position of historical OB/GYN service lines resulted in turf wars over whether the service line should report to nursing or to business development. As gynecology moved out of the hospital in the last decade and some service lines moved into a true population perspective, however, that concern has started to lessen.

Hospital-centric OB/GYN service line positioning is why many organizations fail to realize the potential of non-obstetrical women's services; the category of "women's" doesn't make it beyond gynecology or breast. Internal medicine is pivotal in non-obstetrics women's health. If you are focused on OB/GYN, internal medicine is a specialty you just don't see. That is one of the issues women's hospitals face.

It's difficult to entice the myriad of adult specialists to add an additional site for rounds, so general med-surgical care (particularly high acuity ICU care) tends not to occur in any degree of acuity at women's hospitals. Without that broad base, freestanding women's hospitals in smaller population areas often face rocky financial futures.

The leap into a population-based health service line is a pretty big one, particularly for those who come from OB/GYN. At the true women's level, and particularly within an IDS, the reason operations isn't an inherent responsibility is pretty obvious: Women constitute 60% or more of all admissions and outpatient procedures. If you take operations beyond obstetrics, gynecology and perhaps breast, you're looking at operating 60% or more of the organization.

Population-based service lines like women's health are usually completely strategy and business development, with oversight of marketing, and working with clinicians to achieve clinical care goals. Population-based women's service lines usually have an executive in a business development role, with chief operating officer (COO)–type roles connecting the dots between the service line and operations and back to the service line from operations. This is a structure and perspective that requires substantial relationship skills to accomplish.

Women's Service Line Organizational Structures

The organizational structure of women's health varies considerably by scope. At the hospital level, because the accountability of the service line leader often includes operational accountability, reporting is usually to the chief nurse executive or sometimes to the COO. As the role expands—for a larger hospital or a small system—strategic, business, and/or marketing expectations are added, and the service line leader may report to the COO or the CEO.

At the IDS level, the true women's service line will be focused on strategy, working separately from operations. At this level, what takes place outside of the hospital is far greater than what takes place inside, and the service line executive has to direct strategy for the women's service line across the entire IDS. Reaching at least Charns' matrrix level will be critical.

In the IDS strategy and business development service line model, the service line becomes the glue that organizes systemwide programs around the disciplines to ensure clinical and business outcomes—not to provide another operational layer in the organization.

At the IDS level, if you come from a clinical background, this model guarantees that there will be days when you strongly regret not having operational line authority. Those days will usually involve clinical disasters that never should have happened. Think through your reaction carefully, particularly if you are naturally an "act" personality. If you intervene, build in stabilization outside of your intervention early or you may lose your strategic focus. Your organization depends on you to stay within your role, helping others to grow responsibly into theirs.

Lines of communication

At the IDS level, building successful interfaces with operations is absolutely critical because you will be further away from any hands-on contact you might have had in the past. At the executive level, you need to be at the table. You should have a group of service line peers for hallway consults and joint planning. At the operations and clinical levels, there are multiple ways to maintain communications in both directions. In addition to project teams, examples include the following:

- Regularly scheduled meetings with key clinical and operations staff
- Data flow
- Clinical and/or operational leadership teams
- Including clinical leaders in clinical/business research projects
- Entity planning presentations

Particularly in specialties like obstetrics, neonatology, and pediatrics, there is a role for more intra-IDS service line-provided "consulting" support to help operations directors access the experience and expertise they can't run down a floor to find. This is a critical role for the women's service line, as maternal-newborn, neonatal and pediatric nursing leadership can easily get isolated within any one hospital. Obstetrical units, in general, can get very isolated from the rest of the hospital, and that isolation can lead to significant quality issues and even abusive behavior. With a true women's service line, you will also be providing intra-IDS consulting on gender-based care attributes (see Figure 5.6 for an example of an IDS service line structure with the consultant function).

FIGURE 5.6

EXAMPLE IDS STRATEGIC SERVICE LINE ORGANIZATIONAL STRUCTURE

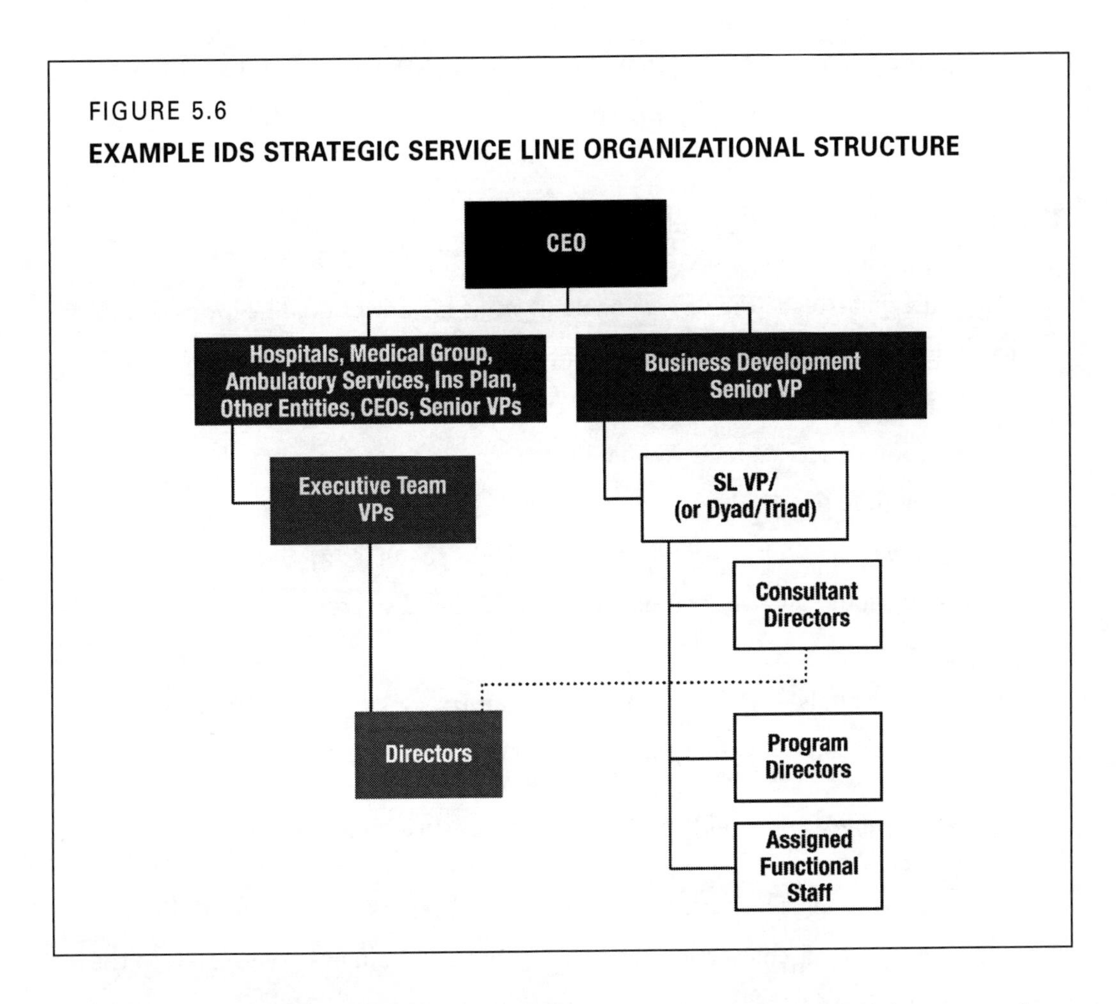

A key role of the service line is to use every tool available to keep the maternal-infant leadership and staff connected and engaged, so they can learn and help each other—no matter how virtual that connection is. Most IDS use call-in and web-based meetings routinely, which is an easy way to stay connected. On-site visits are, of course, required. One of the tricks I learned in early research with IDS women's service line leaders was to get a great car with a great sound system. It can turn travel drudgery into something to look forward to if you are the service line executive in a geographically-spread out IDS.

Who Leads the Service Line?

To identify who leads the service line and what his or her qualifications should be, let's take a look at the requirements of a successful service line, starting with the differences between the traditional functional model of healthcare and the new organization of service lines. While disease-based service lines may have an operational function, the gender-based women's service line cuts across every department you have in your hospital or IDS, which is the most fundamental argument for why it should be at least a matrix organizational structure.

However, hospitals have been functional organizations for a long time. And it's easy to understand why. In a functional organization structure:

- The single command configuration is well-known and therefore comfortable.
- The model is easily understood and has been used for centuries by the military, monarchies, and religious organizations alike. (Note that even these organizations are having difficulty retaining the command-and-control authority they once had.)
- There is a pyramid-like structure with well-defined line and staff functions, easily reinforced with clear-cut organizational charts and job descriptions.
- Each member in the organization has just one supervisor, so it's easy to see who has oversight and proves direction.

- The flow of decisions is usually comfortably downward. Decisions flow from the leader to followers who carry out the directives.
- People are grouped together into functional departments such as nursing, medicine, pharmacy, finance, or marketing.

The problem is that it works well in emergencies and it also worked pretty well back in the day when staff members weren't dealing with the barrage of information we now encounter on a daily basis. Today in healthcare, you have to know and understand how other departments interface with yours. Having a narrow focus can lead to errors on many fronts.

Preventing pharmaceutical errors, for instance, is everyone's problem—from the physician to the nurse to the pharmacist to the computer. If a change occurs in the competitive environment that impacts business development, but not the clinicians, patients will eventually go elsewhere. Now the business problem is also a clinical issue. Likewise, a clinical program glitch that business development or marketing ignore may have systemwide implications. In an era of information excess but decreased resources, everyone needs to be rowing in the same direction.

Finally, even quality is going to a matrix model. For decades, medical research has been limited to a trial involving a single or very few interventions on a single type of patient. With the electronic health record (EHR), multiple interventions in multiple types of patients can be easily and quickly analyzed. An IDS with a fully implemented EHR can give the state government feedback immediately about what population would benefit—and which will not—from proposed statewide initiatives that would have increased costs for all patients. Before the EHR, it would have taken several years after the implementation to discover the cost-benefit ratio.

Most service lines today are at least at Charns' matrix level (refer to Chapter 1). There are many benefits, including:

- There is team coordination and cooperation with a collegial response to a common goal.
- Responses to change in the environment are quicker and more flexible.
- Communication and coordination are increased across the organization.
- The model brings complex skills and experience together from multiple departments. Lifelong learners love this aspect—they are challenged and stimulated more in a matrix than a functional organization, which can increase motivation.
- The matrix structures facilitate teamwork between the business and professional arms of the organization that are required to operate successfully in today's healthcare environment.
- The matrix yields a way of balancing resources and applying them effectively to different projects.
- Staff can (and should) continue to receive professional/technical oversight within their disciplines (see Figure 5.7).

FIGURE 5.7

MATRIX REPORTING ROLES, FUNCTIONAL DEPARTMENTS AND SERVICE LINE

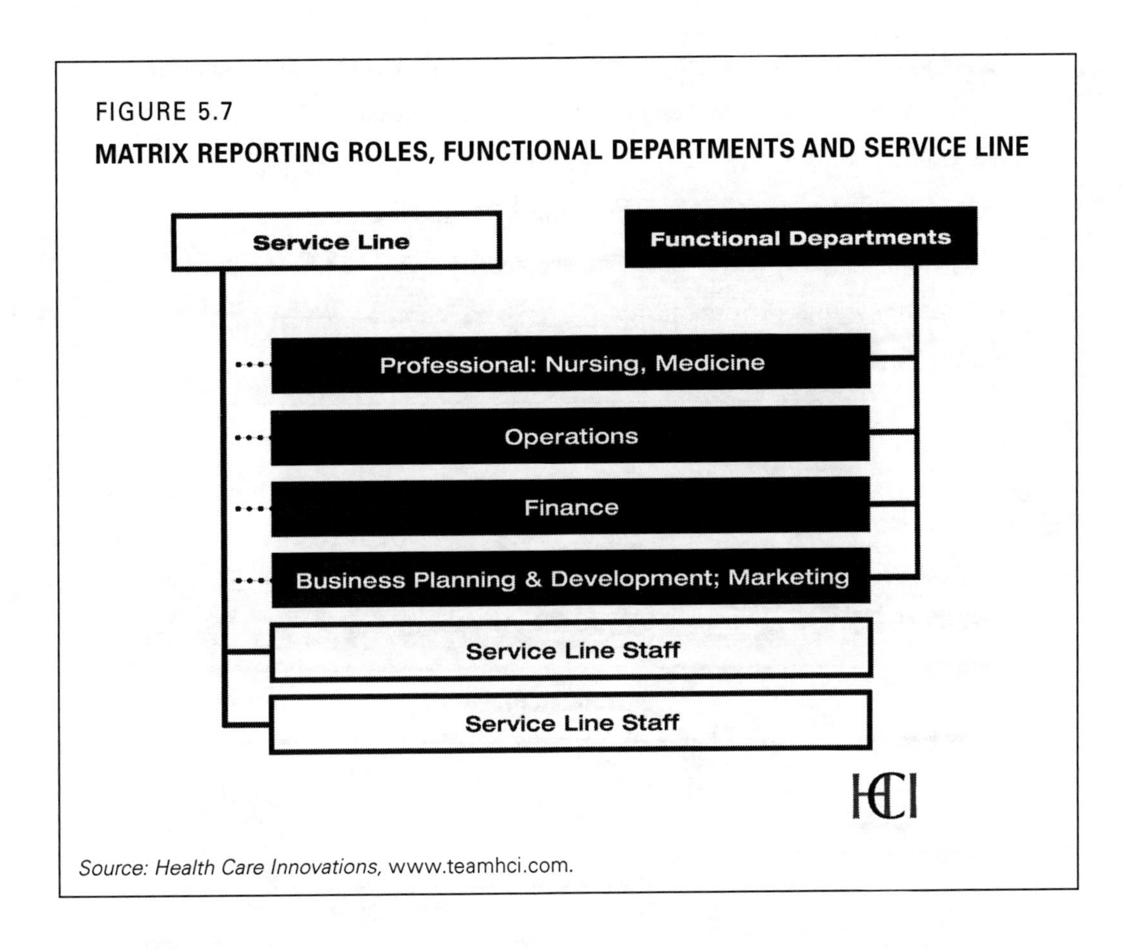

Source: Health Care Innovations, www.teamhci.com.

Achieving accountable care organization (ACO) status will be difficult without at least being at the matrix model. The matrix structure can yield the accountability driving the establishment of ACOs—coordination from prevention to diagnosis to treatment to return to maximum function.

Matrix models have to be grown from the ground up within the organization. They can't just be installed overnight—at least not successfully. Within an IDS, success is accomplished with a structure that balances system goals with the goals of the individual entities, such as hospitals, outpatient centers, the medical group, and insurance plan or payer partners (see Figure 5.8). The service line crosses all these entities within the organization.

FIGURE 5.8

SERVICE LINE COORDINATES WOMEN'S CARE AMONG ALL ENTITIES IN THE IDS

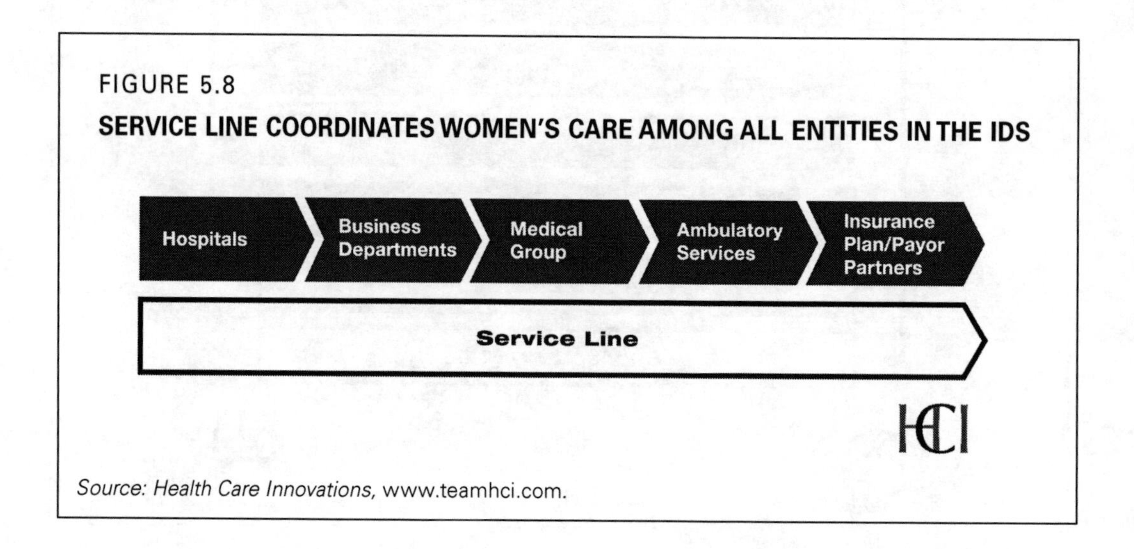

Source: Health Care Innovations, www.teamhci.com.

Attributes

The matrix model is based on the concept of multiple interacting commands, which is the opposite of the traditional functional model. It requires a level of comfort with the concept of having two (or more) bosses. The structure also places a premium on interpersonal skills and human relations training—conflict management, and facilitation and team problem-solving skills. One of the most fundamental criteria for an effective service line leader is outstanding relationship and communication skills.

The leap from clinician or clinical operations to strategy is significant. The characteristics of great clinicians are often the opposite of the characteristics of great service line executives. Once you have been a great clinician, it can be difficult to change direction 180° on the characteristics that made you a great service line leader. Figure 5.9 outlines some of the characteristics of clinical versus service line leaders.

Finally, another important differentiation among women's service line leaders who come from a clinical background is that background itself. Obstetrical and non-obstetrical women's health orientations are very different. Women's health clinicians are rarely completely balanced in both—usually they like either OB or non-obstetrical women's health better than the other. At the service line executive level that tends to balance out in the long run because it has to—both are vital to strategy. Below the executive level there is plenty to do within each. One solution is to use service line directors below the VP level who are specific to each—one for maternal-infant/neonatal another for gynecology and women's health. If those directors can serve as a clinical interface, facilitator, and source for expert operational and clinical solutions, even better.

FIGURE 5.9

CHARACTERISTICS, CLINICIANS AND SERVICE LINE LEADERS

Clinicians	Service line leaders
• Responsive, reactive	• Long-term thinking
• Clear-cut authority, role	• Comfortable with ambiguity
• Functional: Line authority	• Matrix: Authority by relationship
• Manage short time periods	• Manage long time periods
• Enjoy immediate patient and supervisor feedback	• Accustomed to irregular feedback, seek feedback outside service line
• Do whatever asked	• Set priorities to survive
• Take care of everyone	• Take care of self
• Make everyone happy	• Select whom to try to please
• Deep sense of mission	• Adapt to new goals
• Often clinically competitive	• Team support, partnerships critical
• Specialty identity	• Multidisciplinary
• Extremely loyal	• Rethink loyalties, flexible
• Advocate "best" way, caution about new methods	• Inquiry about "best way," search for new, better ways
• Risk adverse	• Risk taker; embrace discomfort
• Concrete, detail-oriented	• Strategic thinking; 30,000 feet
• Passion for great clinical care	• Both quality and business goals
• Passion for the specialty	• Passion for the specialty

Source: Health Care Innovations, www.teamhci.com.

Working the Matrix

Service line models are interdisciplinary at every level. At the IDS level, service line—with organizational and other partners—will be responsible for managing populations through physician and other outpatient care, hospitalization, and return to optimal function.

A key difference between a service line structure and functional departments is that service lines are focused on outcomes, while departments are typically focused on process. Both are important, but it's arguably easier to focus on process without worrying about outcomes. Remember that when outcomes are introduced as being as important as process, there will be conflict and it must be managed.

The successful service line leader has to be focused not just on clinical or business processes, but on balancing outcomes in both. So what is the best background for the service line executive: clinical, business, both, or other?

My observation is that within women's services, the majority of service line executives tend to have a clinical background—more so than disease-based service lines. If they didn't come from a nursing background, they were often in parallel positions elsewhere in the hospital and have strong bonds with nursing.

What matters is having clinical empathy and business acumen—and the ability to pull it together into a meaningful whole for both the organization and the clinicians who care for our families. Miss either clinical empathy or business acumen, and the service line will not thrive. While other service lines may be more finance-oriented, in women's services, the ability to relate to the mission surfaces very quickly.

Acumen in this context refers more to insight than skills, and empathy is the identification with the feelings, thoughts, or attitudes of another. The Japanese have a useful word, "Hai." Loosely translated, it means "yes." But what it really means is "I understand, go on," which is empathy—not necessarily agreement.

Both acumen and clinical empathy are important distinctions. Business acumen doesn't necessarily come with an MHA or MBA, and clinical empathy doesn't necessarily come with an RN or MD/DO. When you look at Figure 5.9, it's clear that no one person could possibly have all the education to know everything there is to know about hospitals, nursing, medical groups, ambulatory care, business functions, and payers. In service lines, it's the outcome that's more important than the professional background or training. I tell our staff that we hire them for their ability to ask questions, not what they already know.

My bias is that it's hard to beat the passion of someone who has chosen a women's clinical care area as his or her first career. The addition of an MHA or MBA or related degree makes it even better—and is pretty much required at the IDS level.

Judith Westphal, the renowned nursing author, writes about resilient organizations and service lines. Westphal notes the requirements of coordination, communication, cooperation, and diplomacy skills in the successful service line executive. She notes nurses have those skills—a unique combination of patient advocacy, networking experience, and mediation among the professions, learned early on.

Whether the nurse is in the executive role in service line, the functional contribution of nursing to the service line as a profession is clear. Nurses are the backbone of patient care, the determinate of professional nursing practice standards and guidelines, the certifier of continuing education and nursing care benchmarks, leaders and contributors to research, and key players in determining best practices and quality of patient—not just nursing—care.

Physicians and Service Line Leadership

The role of physicians in service line leadership is developing rapidly as well. Unlike the past—sort of an era of unrelated cottage healthcare industries—hospitals and physicians are discovering that they really do need each other for an integrated future. The mating dance is happening in earnest, spurred by the push for ACOs or similar full continuum goals. Neither hospitals nor physicians can succeed without the other, and in most organizations voluntary physician staff will continue to far outnumber employed physicians.

There really is nothing like informed physicians and nurses leading objectively balanced, evidence-based quality initiatives from comprehensive planning through implementation and stabilization. If you are the patient, you are thrilled to see it. From the service line executive's perspective, there is nothing more exciting than watching it come together. Ruth Nolan of Geisinger talks about this during the ProvenCare initiative. "It woke me up without my alarm for at least two years," she says.

There are challenges in this new hospital-physician relations arena. On the physician side, the most notable challenge (from the healthcare executive perspective) is overcoming the captain-of-the-ship mentality. Medical schools are starting to realize their role in developing a multidisciplinary team approach to medical education. The traditional authoritative lecture model simply doesn't work anymore. No one physician can represent all the specialty knowledge now available, and there is no one right way for all cases.

Gen X and now Gen Y medical students are pushing the change to interdisciplinary teaching and discourse. They grew up completing team-learning projects from preschool on, unlike their boomer predecessors, who aggressively competed to get their arm up in the air first in class. New medical school curricula are being developed around interdisciplinary teaching and inquiry, as are advanced learner programs such as the new breast fellowships described previously.

The captain-of-the-ship issue is particularly prevalent with "act" physicians, such as surgeons. Crossen, et al., in their article and book on physician leadership, note that clinically outstanding physicians "are not necessarily effective beyond [the clinical area]. When a physician takes off the white coat and is expected to act as a strategist or an administrative and managerial leader...traditional physician leadership skills may actually be counterproductive. A whole new set of skills and perspectives is needed." "Act" physicians also often have the least experience with prevention and rehabilitation, critical functions of the IDS and ACOs.

OB/GYN as a specialty is sometimes described as "half surgical, half medical," and where an OB/GYN falls on this divide often outlines at least the initial approach he or she will bring to service line leadership and management. Surgeons of any type are often admired as decisive; however, strategic leadership requires more consensus-building than decisiveness. As a result of the extremely litigious environment in obstetrics, many OB/GYNs are also fairly risk-adverse. Leadership is full of risk, and the degree to which a leader is willing to take strategic risks can separate success from failure.

Other challenges on both sides of the physician and healthcare executive aisles include the following:

- There is a very different sense of time from thought to action
- Each answers to a completely different constituency
- The bottom line has different meanings for each
- There is a different concept of value

Authors Craig Holm and Joseph S. Bujak, MD, do a terrific job describing the differences between physicians and healthcare executives, as well as what the two have in common, such as the quest for quality.

When you get to the end of the requirements list for a service line executive, what emerges is the need to merge clinical and business outcomes and knowledge. Neither is more important than the other, and without a clear direction and achievable strategy, service becomes only an additional layer of management.

Achieving that balance depends largely on the scope and goals of the service line leadership position, and the skills of the other people on the team. No one can possibly know everything; however, there has to be accountability—and the more people involved, the more diffuse the accountability. Whatever the leadership model, the dual business and clinical outcomes must be achieved.

Positioning the Service Line

This will be driven entirely by the goals of the organization, informed—with valuable information—by the service line.

Within healthcare organizations, justification for a women's health service line sometimes requires a bit more informing than that required for the three high altars of healthcare: cancer, heart, and orthopedics (or neurosciences, more recently). It's easy to say that the need to explain the financial value of women's services is a gender issue, but like many so-called gender issues, it's just as often a generational issue. Most decision-makers in organizations—senior executive and board members—tend not be of childbearing age. It makes sense that heart attacks, cancer, and orthopedics are of more immediate concern to them than babies.

And while boomer women have changed the world as they worked their way through the decades, it is only in the last decade that they have started to populate senior executive and board ranks in numbers. Those numbers are still very low: A 2008 report indicated that women still held only 15% or less of board positions in industry. It's definitely not just healthcare.

A financial bias also exists from the old revenue heydays. Today's data often don't bear out those perceptions—and really didn't then, either. But diseases are easier to track financially; it takes more work to track the value of a women's service line, or a men's service line, for that matter.

However, even on a departmental financial analysis, the neonatal contribution margin in a surgical Level III NICU on an occupied bed basis is as good as or better than inpatient heart surgery. Both outlier high-risk maternal and neonatal care can raise the entire case-mix index of a hospital very quickly. And then, of course, there is the overall site decision power of the female consumer—but that's something not everyone enjoys hearing on a regular basis, so be sparing with that one.

If the influence of the high altars is strong at your hospital or system, women's services might be devalued. On the other hand, it might just be underrepresented by data, making your system uninformed about the ways engaging women can make the organization much more successful. It's up to you to demonstrate those data. Make sure your data are presented at the same time as that of other service lines; force the issue if, for instance, the only data shown or reported are about other service lines. You will need to spend time learning the data and digging to find the source (and making sure it's accurate), but you will be in the presentation, and you will likely be surprised at how well you compare.

Life would be easier if we could just say women's services is the right thing to focus on, but no one else gets to do that—and this is definitely the era of information and analysis.

Another tip is to develop easy-to-remember factual blurbs about the value of your services. I try to pluck out single numbers that executives can remember easily, and repeat them often. When those statistics are quoted back to you, you are headed in the right direction. A word of caution: Make sure finance or other sources agree that number is real. You don't need to lose credibility.

While you have great power to enhance it, the baseline institutional valuing of women's services is important in determining your starting point. On a bad day, no one feels valued, but it's important to put some objectivity around what is otherwise a pretty subjective topic. Based on more than 800 consulting projects here and abroad, I put together some of the symptoms I have seen in organizations that devalue women's services, undervalue it, or value it (Figure 5.10). Not all hold true for every organization, but you will get the idea.

Knowing where your organization is, realistically, will help shape your plan and your analysis and translations of what you do.

If you seriously feel your organization is significantly toward the left of this scale, don't worry about it—at least not yet. But it does mean that you will have more translating to do.

FIGURE 5.10

ENVIRONMENTAL SCAN: ORGANIZATIONAL VALUING OF WOMEN'S SERVICES

Devalue	Undervalue	Value
• Not the market share leader and declining market share in OB and/or gynecology • Women's not in slated institutional priorities and not understood to be a priority • Few or no women in executive positions outside nursing or religious roles • Paired with behavioral health, examples include: in executive reports and when left in old facility when other services moved to a new one • Open negativity without leader correction • Finance-driven institution • History of attempts to close the service • Dilapidated, outdated, noncompetitive, or unfriendly facilities • OB/GYNs: low priority in physician pecking order (e.g., OR use) • Lack of development/marketing budget • Either no director or a director without budget, accountability, or authority	• Doing well but no one knows details (accomplishments, market share, margin) • Not stated in institutional priorities, but understood to be a priority • Women in some leadership positions outside of nursing and religious roles • Facility and equipment renovation—five years ago, but competitive • Seen as obligatory service—part of mission, but not margin; usually little understanding of downstream referral value or potential of higher acuity revenues • History of having done well in OB in the past, but now facing financial difficulty, refocusing on finance and revenues • Often a formal or informal "go-to" person for the service line, or recent history of director who may have recently been let go at same time as other directors due to finances	• Market leader or growing market share • Recognition regionally and nationally • Solid female representation in leadership positions outside nursing or religious roles • Active product development and marketing • Everyone understands and speaks strategic importance as business driver and revenue source • Women's is in top five stated strategic priorities for institution • Well-maintained, up to date, female-friendly facilities and equipment • Market-driven institutional with solid finances • Usually includes higher revenue aspects of OB (NICU, maternal fetal medicine, women's subspecialists) • Financially stable organizations with long-term view • Dedicated service line executive(s) with a known budget, formal hospital- or systemwide authority, and accountability for outcomes

Source: Health Care Innovations, www.teamhci.com.

Whether your organization is to the left or the right on Figure 5.10, as an executive, you will spend much of your time translating what you do into language that your market—your internal market—understands. If the organization is financially driven, that means translating what you do into numbers—developed with and verified by finance—that the organization will understand. It also can mean teaching downstream financial analysis to the organization. If you are in the subspecialty business, downstream analysis is critical. While departmental finance still dominates healthcare, downstream analysis is becoming easier to do every day and is critical to figuring out the relationship of the moving parts in a matrix organization.

And while you are translating, also be informing the values and focus of your organization. Report what's needed in your organization, but don't hesitate to teach about what should also be important. Industry has figured out that women are the market. Healthcare knows it but does not always live it. Quality outcomes, patient satisfaction, referring physician satisfaction—these and other benchmarks are those measured by today's organizations. You already know these are important to women's services, so make sure you speak your outcomes in a language that is internally understood and expected.

Besides adding positive energy and enthusiasm, one of the most powerful attributes a service line leader needs to have is the ability to translate what they are doing into the language of the buyer—internal or external.

Successful service lines are always market-driven. Market-driven is when your strategy is guided by trends in your market and the needs of your customers with value-added expertise from you—the part the customer doesn't know they don't know. The opposite is product-driven, in which your products are pushed by what you want to produce or by current capacity. For product-driven, I've been using the example of some American car makers (mentioning no names) for 20 years. For market-driven examples, I've used the names of some Japanese car makers. No corporation is perfect, but it's amazing how that slide didn't change over two decades, providing excellent examples of the influence and long-term viability of unchanging corporate cultures.

Being internally market-driven as an executive means meeting the needs of the organization—supporting the strategy of the organization within your own service line. Women's service lines that go merrily off on their own always end up in trouble. If it doesn't work for the organization, it won't work in the long run for you or for the women to whom you provide services.

Whatever the organization needs to succeed is what you have to provide first. After that, your role is to inform. The organization doesn't know what you know. That's why you're there. Your job is to help move your organization and your community along the scale of enlightenment about the possibilities of women becoming more engaged with your hospital or system. If the scale of perfection is from one to 10, no one moves from a two to a 10 overnight. You move the twos to threes, the fives to sixes, and so on. It's incremental, and every year you have the opportunity to move it a little further along.

Although that may sound slow, there are many advantages to an incremental approach. One of the most significant is that the service line doesn't get too far ahead of the hospital or healthcare system, which is a dangerous position. It's really not much different than raising kids. You can push a four-year-old to act like a 10-year-old, but their friends won't come along so peer pressure shows up quickly. And eventually the child will decompensate, which is never pretty. Another advantage to the incremental approach is that it gives the service line the chance to stabilize one set of changes before undertaking another.

The Business Plan

The outline of a business plan is readily available from many sources, including fill-in-the-blank business plans on the Internet. The general components include the following:

- Executive summary
- Current status
- Goals and objectives
- Tactics and costs
- Return on investment (in brand, volumes, and dollars)
- How you will monitor progress

The best source for your business plan template, however, will be within your organization. What format is preferred by those to whom you report? Ask for examples of outstanding internal business plans and use one of those templates.

You will absolutely want support from at least two departments as you write your business plan: finance and decision support. ("Finance," by the way, is a product-driven term. "Decision support" is market-driven. One pushes a product required by the organization—all the routine financial analysis we all need to stay alive. Decision support provides what you, their market, need to get where you're going. Finance is usually also part of the decision-support group, and finding a finance person who understands the difference can make corporate life more rewarding.)

Finally, consider reducing the key elements of your overall strategy and plan to a one-page slide. You will find it useful almost every week. Have one for obstetrics-neonatal/newborn, and another for non-obstetrical women's services. See the general idea in Figure 5.11. Use very few words and use symbols whenever possible.

FIGURE 5.11
EXAMPLE OF IDS STRATEGY-AT-A-GLANCE

	System	Payers	Medical group	Hosp A	Hosp B	Hosp C
Quality focus						
Brand focus						
Share focus						
Revenue focus						
Objective 1						
Objective 2						
Objective 3						
Objective 4						

Resource allocation

I noted that if you felt your hospital or system was to the left of the devalue-value grid (Figure 5.10), you shouldn't worry—at least not yet.

There are some danger signals for service line leaders. Working in an institution that stays, or changes to, the far left of that grid will be a problem in the long run. Another danger sign is lack of access to resources.

It is the institution's accountability to ensure you get the meaningful data, information, and support you need to achieve your goals. It is the service line leader's responsibility to get that information—and help the institution know what you need and why you need it. About 90% of the time, when I hear a service line leader say he or she can't get that data, the data are available, but hard to find. The service line leader may not know how to ask the right question or how to find the person who has the information. Often it's as simple as asking for data from the wrong department, for example, asking finance for planning data or asking planning for finance data.

There are inherent challenges when working with what I call the "linear sciences" such as finance, legal, and planning. The best of these professionals go very carefully from one step to the other. You appreciate that when it's your finances they are reporting.

Many service line leaders, however, are more intuitive—less A to B and more, say, A to Q. Don't expect good linear professionals to follow that bouncing ball without your help. Talk it through with them and help them figure out what you need.

And make sure you listen to them. The value of the linear sciences is that they will find the gaps and traps you have not anticipated.

The people to look for in these linear sciences are those who can think both in a linear fashion and get a sense of where the ball is bouncing—see where you are headed and the data needed to test the theory. Make these translators your new best friends at work.

While you will need access to resources, most of the access will be a part of a full-time employee (FTE), not an entire FTE assigned to the service line. That doesn't mean it won't be tempting to hire complete FTEs, and there will definitely be times when the access you need is not necessarily what you can get. It will be a balance to discover at what point you likely need full-time support.

All of these professionals are part of functional departments for a reason: to keep up their functional skills and knowledge. Bringing them full time into the service line often can cut that link, limiting their upward mobility and potentially the skills brought to the service line. The benefits need to be weighed against the risks.

Hospitals and health systems use different methods to assign functional support to service lines. Sometimes it's formal and sometimes it isn't. What's important is that, over time, you feel you can get the support you need. These are most of the areas in which you will need functional support, listed alphabetically—not by priority:

- Change science gurus like organizational development, Six Sigma–certified green/black belts, productivity, and human factor professionals

- Facility planning and redevelopment
- Finance, including current status, estimates, and scenario development
- Legal, with an emphasis on healthcare compliance issues and contracting
- Management information services: hard, soft, and cloud
- Marketing, including research, advertising, and public relations
- Operations
- Organizational development
- Planning, both business and regulatory
- Quality and safety
- R&D specific to the service line, both clinical and business
- Revenue cycle, including pricing, contracting, coding, billing, and reimbursement

The larger the organization, the more likely the organization will have these functional departments on board. The smaller, the more often you will run into access barriers. Regardless of the size of your organization, when you run into access issues, there are a couple of options. Consider the issue you are currently facing and where it falls in the project stages.

1. Who do you know in your organization that has successfully managed issues like this before, even if that isn't their primary function?

2. What books or journals might provide that information?

3. What does Google (or another search engine) offer on the topic?

4. Who do you know is talented at management of the project phase you're in, and can help you get through what will be intuitive for them?

5. Is this something you will need long term? If not, can you borrow or buy that talent for a short term?

Skills most often contracted for outside the organization include legal, service line–specific research and development, marketing and public relations, and problem solving, coaching, and change management for specific situations.

Budget for kickoff and maintenance

Every service line leader's budget will be different based on the organization's expectations of service line. There is likely a budgeting template that you can—or must—use. If you are a hospital service line leader with primarily an operational focus, you will have a budget to cover those operations. If you are the service line leader in an IDS, your budget will likely include portions of FTEs in several functional department and any operational unit for which you have accountability, and likely full or partial control over business development and/or marketing budgets.

If you're kicking off a new women's service line, one area where you might not have historical data to lean on may be marketing, specifically including public relations, not just advertising. In obstetrics, consistent marketing is more important to service line viability than perhaps in any other service line.

To determine a marketing budget for the first time, the steps are similar to developing a business plan. You will want to develop a strategic marketing plan that clearly spells out objectives and tactics, and that presents easy measures of where you are now and where you want to be, as well as costs and return on that investment. The development of a marketing budget is another place where finance can help you in justification. For instance, the cost of marketing can be compared to the ROI of incremental volumes in the area you are marketing—or the loss to another hospital or system if you are not competitively positioned.

Then ask two or three marketing firms for their estimates of kickoff and maintenance costs. The two are very different. Kickoff costs will be 50%–100% more than maintenance, depending on your market size, complexity, and media mix. The size of your market greatly affects your marketing budget. The cost of marketing in a city of 100,000 is nothing compared to penetrating the market of an area of a million or more. Compare the estimates. Probe the differences. Don't be afraid to ask questions or to really hone in on how the results of a recommended marketing tactic can be measured over the long run in brand, volumes, or margin. It needs to make sense to you, or it won't make sense to anyone else.

Summary

Every hospital and every IDS is changing as a result of external pressures and events; understanding yourself, your team, your internal environment, and the organization's expectations are just as important as knowing the external environment. Change is incremental. Very few people have the opportunity to start from scratch, overnight, not having to deal with any prior organizational history.

As you embark on starting a service line or taking an existing service line up to a new level, some of the internal variables you will need to consider are the following:

- Where your hospital or health system is in system development. The needs of service line will be different at different stages.
- Whether you have the right people in place for the goals to be accomplished. Particularly as systems evolve, new talent may be required at higher levels of function.
- Potential service line responsibilities, accountabilities, and organizational structures, which should match system development. New structure will be built around at least the matrix model, with care not to try to shape the new service line model back into a functional model.
- Characteristics, experience, and leadership qualities of the service line leader, again driven by system needs and accountabilities.
- New structures and ways of organizing around matrix to provide value to the organization—not create redundancies.
- Working with functional departments to get the support the service line needs to achieve the work of the organization and the service line.
- Components of strategic planning, and who can help you flush out the details, as well as an overview of how budgeting fits in.

References

Bujak, Joseph S. *Inside the Physician Mind: Finding Common Ground With Doctors.* American College of Healthcare Executives (ACHE): Health Administration Press, 2008.

Crosson, F.J., Weiland, Alan, Berenson, Robert. "Physicians as Leader: Physician Leadership 'Group Responsibility' as Key to Accountability in Medicine." *The Permanente Journal.* Summer 2004, Vol. 8, Excerpted from *Toward a 21st Century Health System: The Contributions and Promise of Prepaid Group Practice* by Alain Enthoven and Laura Tollen, editors. Jossey-Bass/A Wiley Imprint. April 2004,

Epstein, Andrew L., and Bard, Marc A. "Selecting Physician Leaders for Clinical Service Lines: Critical Success Factors." *Academic Medicine* 83 (2008): 226–234.

Holm, Craig. *Next Generation Physician-Health System Partnerships.* ACHE: Health Administration Press, 2000.

Jain, Anshu K., et al. "Fundamentals of Service Lines and the Necessity of Physician Leaders." *Surgical Innovation* 13 (2006): 136–144.

Nolan, Ruth. Interviews with author. 2010.

Rosenberg, Sheli. "Why Aren't There More Women on Boards?" *Bloomberg Businessweek* (April 2008). *www.businessweek.com/managing/content/apr2008/ca2008048_611396.htm?chan=top+news_top+news+index_managing.*

Westphal, Judith A. "Resilient Organizations: Matrix Model and Service Line Management." *Journal of Nursing Administration* 35 (2005): 414–419.

CHAPTER 6

Finance and Marketing

When it comes to defining and proving service line value, finance and marketing should go hand in hand. In women's health, "delicious distractions" abound. The opportunities are endless: from spas to retail to dancing for heart health to increasing subspecialty practices to building primary care. Every possible approach has some merit. At the end of each year, and every three- to five-year period, you should be able to demonstrate what you accomplished, how it supported your organization, and how it improved healthcare for women.

Defining Service Line Value

Many organizations have goals that fall into one of three categories: brand, volumes, or margin. Mitch Galloway, of Galloway Consulting, has a great, easy-to-remember model for sorting through these opportunities (see Figure 6.1).

FIGURE 6.1
DEFINE AND MEASURE VALUE

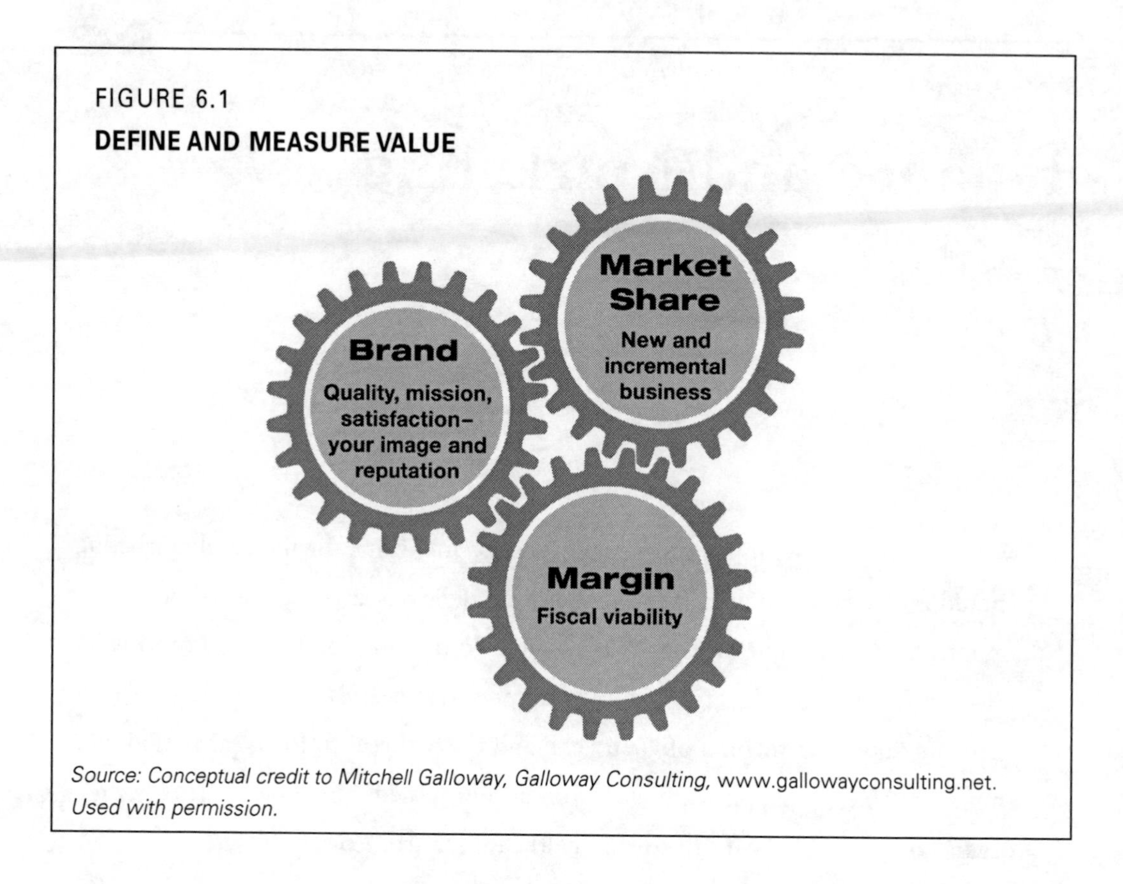

Source: Conceptual credit to Mitchell Galloway, Galloway Consulting, www.gallowayconsulting.net. *Used with permission.*

In Figure 6.1, brand includes quality, mission, patient, and physician satisfaction—everything that creates the public image or reputation of your institution. Volume is market share, and margin is what—in the long run—keeps all of us in business.

The following are expanded definitions for each category:

- **Brand:** A product or service distinguished by distinctive characteristics. It is the mental representation of your company and is often tied to an icon or other symbol/emblem of the company. In today's world, it includes quality as reported—not just claimed.

- **Volumes (market share):** The specific percentage of total industry sales of a particular product achieved by a single company in a given period. For example, the percentage of inpatients in obstetrics in your entire service area over a specific time period.

- **Margin:** In Galloway's original model, this category was called revenue. I use margin: the amount of funds available—the contribution—to overhead or fixed operating costs and profit after variable costs have been covered.

In this model, improved brand leads to improved market share, which leads to improved margin, which ultimately creates a better brand position, and so on. Galloway notes his group is now seeing brand improvements from quality result in incremental margin from pay for performance (P4P) initiatives.

The benefits of this model are its simplicity and the fact that you can work it both coming and going. You can begin with the goal of wanting to improve your volumes or margin and work backward into the vectors that create or limit you. This is one of the ways Galloway demonstrates the value of the model, first identifying major factors leading to positive or negative changes in each, then the causative vectors.

It works well the other way around as well. When a delicious distraction is proposed for your consideration, you can evaluate the merits in relationship to this model, and determine how it will have a *measurable* impact in one of the three categories. If you can't see where it will measurably improve your position, you might consider that opportunity for further study later on, perhaps for the next fiscal year.

And, importantly, this model gives healthcare leaders categories through which they can demonstrate value. Just about everything you do can be measured in one of these categories. Market share and margin are obvious. But brand is actually more measurable than most people think—quality can be measured and reported, and mission can be as well. Overall, brand is measured regularly by most institutions with market-area image studies, which ask questions like, "Which health system is best for women's care?"

To measure value in each category, organizations can use the following metrics:

- Brand
  - Improvement in image and visibility surveys
  - Reach to new populations (e.g., educational offerings, screenings)
  - New charity care opportunities (often applicable to an explicit organizational charity goal)
  - Number of community outreach visits
- Volumes
  - Incremental market share in target services

  - Increased volumes in target services
  - Increased referrals for screenings for diagnostic services

- Margin
  - Improved margins in target services, whether from new/incremental revenues or decreased costs

Leaders shouldn't think of the measures as only being related to obstetrics or gynecology. These are much more broadly applicable.

For instance, in most image/visibility surveys, you can sort responses by male and female. If you have taken strategic advantage of partnering sponsorship opportunities and screenings specific to women's heart, for instance, you should see the needle moving among female respondents. It's exciting to be able to demonstrate that the overall hospital or integrated delivery system (IDS) brand moved because you increased the brand among women, as in Figure 6.2, an example graph based on a similar story at a real system.

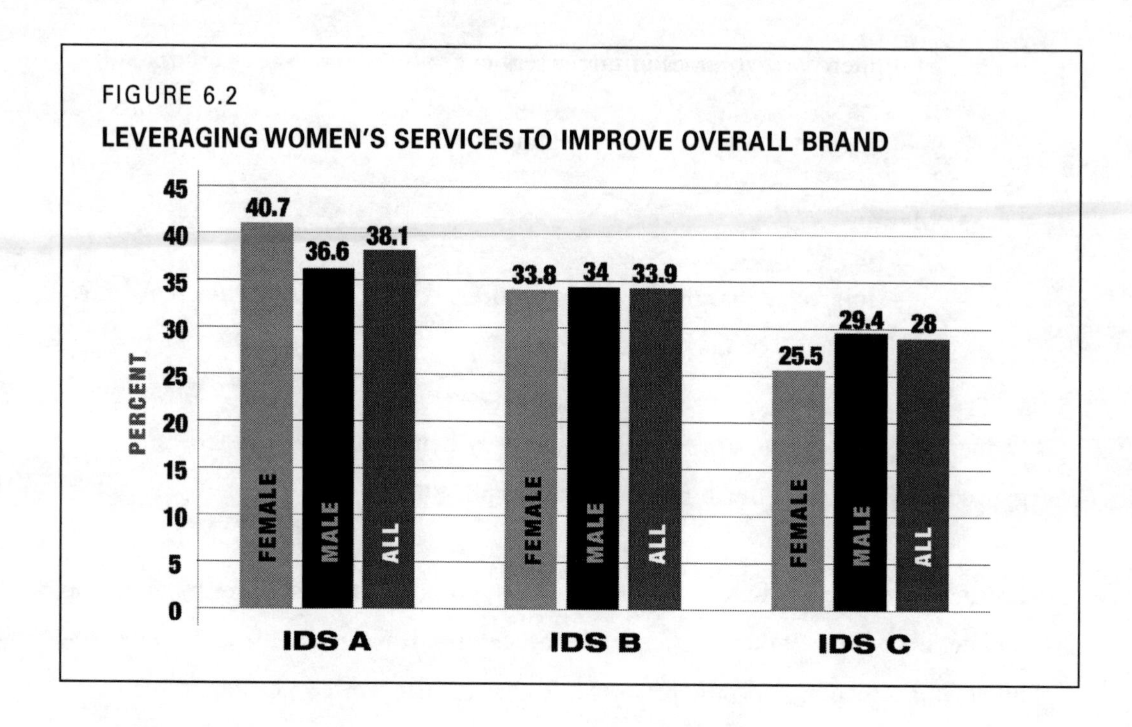

The example IDS A in Figure 6.2 improved its brand as measured from year one to year two in an image survey. The IDS examined year two findings in more depth looking at the breakout of results by gender of respondent. Female recognition of the brand was what led the resurgence of the brand. That preference followed substantial work on a gender-specific approach to the heart product line being measured.

If you are spending your money effectively, particularly if you have focused on a specific campaign for two to three years, you should be able to move the needle.

Brand is influenced most quickly by marketing and public relations efforts and more slowly by word-of-mouth. Brand recognition leads to volumes. Volumes help brand preference, but not much. For example, brand might be measured by a random sample of 600 people in your metropolitan area—only one or two of them might actually have received care at your institution.

This type of focus and analysis is where finance and marketing merge to support and inform your goals and tactics. In marketing, in particular, you can spend a lot of money very quickly without demonstrable results. When considering a new program, whether in marketing or overall development, ask, "How does this build or support the goals of the organization in brand, volumes, or margin?" Then ask, "What measurable results in one of those categories will justify this expenditure?"

If what you're doing is achieving results, you can always find a way to measure and report it. And if you can't see results in at least the brand category, you should probably reconsider your tactic.

That observation begs a discussion about tactics, related to delicious distractions. Many of us in women's service line leadership positions are women. One of the dangers we face is planning subjectively, rather than objectively. This issue is critical to successful women's health service line planning. Being a woman means we likely know a fair amount about what women like us want and need—although we are admittedly biased by virtue of being a healthcare professional, a very big and often unrecognized bias.

The problem is that there are many more women out there who are not like us. They are not in healthcare. For example, they may be older, younger, more liberal, more conservative, or of a different ethnicity or culture.

There are some very expensive opportunities in women's health, and someone will always like at least one of them. The question is whether there are enough of those "someones" to yield a return on your investment, and whether the investment will improve brand, volumes, or margin.

This is where research comes in handy. Know your market from the market's perspective, not just yours. The only way to be market-driven is to come at your tactics from the market's perspective. Your perspective as a woman is interesting, but your market-driven, evidence-based leadership is essential.

Margin

Margin, in this context, is net revenue (reimbursement) minus variable costs. Some institutions call this contribution margin or variable-contribution margin. On a profit-loss statement, look in the column after the variable cost column but before direct costs column.

What you are *not* looking for is contribution margin calculated *after* fixed and indirect costs. Fixed costs should not affect product development decisions because they cannot be changed. And the good news—and the reason to focus on contribution margin—is that unit-fixed costs decline as volumes increase.

When looking at profit-loss statements, the tendency of many executives is to go straight to the bottom line. There are two problems with this. One is that hardly anything makes money once all the direct and indirect costs are applied, so pretty quickly you start wanting to keep the radiology department but get rid of all those cost-consuming, irritating patients. (Reviewing the profit-loss statements of your organization's 20 most profitable ventures can help shed light on this topic.)

The second issue is that the bottom line doesn't tell you what will happen if you increase volumes, which is likely what your job entails. Low profit/loss per case is too often used to prevent expansion of services or to leverage cost-savings initiatives. Although cost savings is absolutely part of your job, no one has ever cost-cut themselves into long-term profitability. The larger part of your job is to create new volumes—and using the contribution margin will allow you to test that.

There's always disgruntlement with how costs are applied. That's a universal truth, like taxes and death. Don't get caught up in the quagmire of defining how costs are assigned. That conversation rarely goes anywhere. Assume costs are assigned evenly by your organization across the board. Move on to the possibilities of improving margins.

MAKING FINANCE YOUR NEW BFF

It is common to get frustrated when working with others who don't understand what language (medical, technology, or finance) we're speaking. It's important to remember that you are in your position because you are an expert in your field. Likewise, your coworkers are also in their positions because they are experts in their fields. The very best advice I can give anyone new to the service line leadership role, or advancing up the IDS food chain, is to make finance your BFF or best friend forever.

Financial analysts have to be linear thinkers to be good—as with the legal profession, the devil is in the details in their profession. If you are fairly intuitive, you may well have a Myers-Briggs work style clash with detailed linear thinking. That doesn't make you right and them wrong. Think whole-brain and get to know them. You will likely be pleasantly surprised once you do that, and they will appreciate someone who works with them rather than blaming them for any and all bad news on financial analyses. They are simply doing the same thing you are—helping the organization to be successful.

Beyond Department Analysis

Departmental finance has always been the standard in hospital finance. The bottom line for every department in the hospital is measured predictably on a regular basis.

The functional departmental arrangement of hospitals has been around for a long time, and the interdisciplinary matrix model in hospitals—and academic medicine—is finally catching up to how other industries operate.

Saying "departmental finance has always been the standard in hospital finance" is to say that healthcare finance has been arranged around the needs of the functional organizational model. But the conservative profession of hospital finance is starting to make significant progress toward standardized support of the matrix. And to be fair, supporting the matrix model is a large shift for a profession that prides itself on precision.

Historically, in hospital finance, you could use standard financial analysis to demonstrate that the only departments that made money in a hospital were the lab, pharmacy, radiology, and central supply. So if you wanted to really make money, you just needed to close down everything else.

We have moved beyond that point and now we can look at patient encounters as well as departmental analysis. Cost accounting improved as well. Diagnosis-related groups (DRG) can be grouped into DRG-based service lines, and analysis of those groupings of DRGs is commonly available as well. Analysis of outpatient services has improved too. In most hospitals, it is easy to pull the patient records by physician and, within minutes, see the total revenues, costs, and margin of any one physician, procedure, or group of DRGs. You can draw a lot of conclusions from today's financial analysis.

But what usually isn't easily and regularly available at most hospitals or health systems is any kind of analysis of downstream revenue. Yet DRGs don't always work. For instance, you can't follow neonatal ICU (NICU) use with DRGs. You can track sick babies, but you can't track NICU admissions. And, of course, if you take the OB/GYN DRGs, that analysis doesn't tell you how the admissions track with neonatal DRGs, let alone NICU admissions, which sometimes bolsters a mental mind-set in finance or operations that maybe babies really do come from storks.

In addition, much of the downstream data is laborious to gather, has to come from multiple sources, and is too often dependent on human intervention. Even if you get the data, it usually results in a partial picture anyway. Trying to track patient encounters resulting from a seminar is a great example of doing a lot of one-off work in a lot of places only to end up with more questions than answers.

In healthcare, we also have privacy barriers to contend with. Consumers are smarter about how their data can be used and reluctant to give identifying data that can easily be tracked through the system, such as Social Security numbers. And at some point in downstream analysis, you usually have to make a subjective attribution on something—like what percentage of new admissions likely came from marketing versus the addition of new physicians or some other factor. That's not always comfortable for financial professionals who take pride in being able to track tangible numbers and identifying causative relationships. Finally, the person who makes the subjective attribution usually doesn't have a degree in finance—it's the service line leader. Even though they know the service line and how it works, it is uncomfortable for finance leaders to follow that path of thinking without clear-cut evidence—although it's a great example of matrix in action.

We don't always think through the value of what we're trying to prove, which means finance or other decision-support services could spend a lot of time and still not get you what you need. For example, many people still ask me how to prove that if you capture a woman for her first pregnancy, you will get her as a patient for life. I don't advise spending much time on that because I don't believe it's as applicable in this very mobile age with regular insurance plan changes, although it may have been when this theory first surfaced about 40 years ago.

As women move through the stages of life, they will usually change homes, and the call of a hospital close to home remains a powerful draw. A woman may also change providers as she matures. There is enough market research to show a woman's level of insurance coverage is more important than staying with a favorite provider for her lifelong needs, particularly for high-cost care such as inpatient services. The value of the woman in any given year as the insurance plan and site-of-care decision-maker, is more than enough to offset worrying about her being a lifelong loyalist.

The issue is that departmental analysis simply does not tell the story you need as the service line executive. In fact, huge mistakes can be made in business decisions using only departmental analysis. A classic and very timely example everyone is dealing with right now is employment of physicians. At least with subspecialists, employment would often look delusional from a medical group perspective. In most cases, all the costs are all in the medical group (a department), and the entire margin is elsewhere—in the hospital and outpatient centers. If future planning looks only at departmental finance, you would rarely employ a subspecialist.

While most contemporary financial analysis is based on process or departments, business development decisions are focused on outcomes, not processes. Downstream analysis will drive much of your decision-making.

Downstream analysis should be used on just about every significant business development idea that does not increase volumes or margin immediately. You will want to determine where it does affect your goals. For instance, downstream analysis is ideal to give focus to relationship marketing.

Some of the clinical or business development ideas you want to study are simple. Others are complex and involve financial risk. For the more complex, risky decisions, careful analysis done in concert with finance is required. For the simple ones, make the analysis as simple as you can. It's easy to be wound up in a complex method when some simple numbers would do the trick.

Examples of downstream revenue and value

Value of prenatal classes

This example is a very simple one, proving the value of prenatal classes. Those of us who come from the clinical side know this is the right thing to do. Parents need tremendous support before, during, and after birth to have a successful birth and parenting experience. But from a departmental perspective (childbirth education department), classes simply look like costs.

On the other hand, if you demonstrate that starting and marketing classes increased deliveries—not that hard to demonstrate—you can claim the downstream revenue or margin from those admissions as justification for the classes. That new revenue shows up in hospital departments, although it originated from your classes.

You just found a way to make the justification a lot easier for those who don't understand your field the way you do.

The sources of data you need for this analysis are usually business development and/or finance. In the new accountable care organization (ACO) era, there will be a justification that appeals to even more of us in women's health, and that is that classes should shift to demonstrating how to prevent complications. For instance, teaching the Bishop Score to parents—including use of the Apple® app that predicts the likelihood of a cesarean using the Bishop Score—is a great way to help Gen X and Y mothers rethink elective induction. Not many health systems are asking for that validation right now, but it's coming.

Value of telemedicine

This example was published as part of a 2005 conference on telemedicine, held by the American Telemedicine Association.

A large children's hospital reported the before-and-after results of providing telemedicine echocardiograms, which are pretty simple to do. However, with departmental analysis only—and a general lack of knowledge about the power of telemedicine—efforts to initiate something like this will often run into institutional barriers.

The hospital demonstrated more than 50% increase in new business, with incremental downstream revenues of almost $3 million in departments downstream of where the echocardiograms were read, particularly in surgery.

The source of data for this analysis comes from finance and service line leaders.

Value of employing a subspecialist

Here is a case example of something more complex: justifying the hiring of a subspecialist. This is one of my favorites because it demonstrates the juxtaposition of traditional financial analysis and downstream analysis.

This analysis was done to justify adding a third subspecialist in a particular subspecialty of OB/GYN. The exact type doesn't matter; what you want to look at are the categories of analysis.

Subspecialists are pretty expensive positions to fill. Even median salaries are often in the $300,000–$600,000+ range per year. Add another 25%–30% for benefits and the fact that you always need at least two subspecialists for on-call coverage, which is really still below what is needed for lifestyle balance, and you have an investment not taken casually.

In this example, there was existing internal data for a downstream "look-back." If you don't have existing data, there are still ways to get the information necessary. You might have a friend in another health system who can provide the data points, or you can usually put it together yourself from various sources on incidence of disease, admissions, outpatient cases, and types from industry reports.

The already-existing two subspecialist physicians were being reported on a departmental basis as two of the least profitable admitters in the entire hospital system, with a terrible payer mix. The service line leader was able to add an asterisk to that report showing that the particular subspecialty supported other specialties, rather than directly admitting patients. The only time the subspecialty ended up being the admitting physician at this institution was when a true disaster occurred with a walk-in patient, who was also likely uninsured. Then the subspecialists became the admitting physician of record—a situation guaranteed to not show great financial performance as the *admitting* physician.

A better analysis was clearly required. Working together, the service line executive and the finance department did the most difficult (and most precise) type of look-back. To establish a baseline for future reviews, they actually pulled patient records (electronically). All patient records associated with subspecialist care in the office were pulled and followed for the prior year. Because of the high cost of salaries, the office practice was a money loser as well—although it was the first place the patients of these subspecialists were seen.

The results, as shown in Figure 6.3, found that the subspecialty returned a 5.5:1 benefit-cost ratio to the IDS—a very different outcome than "the least profitable admitting physician."

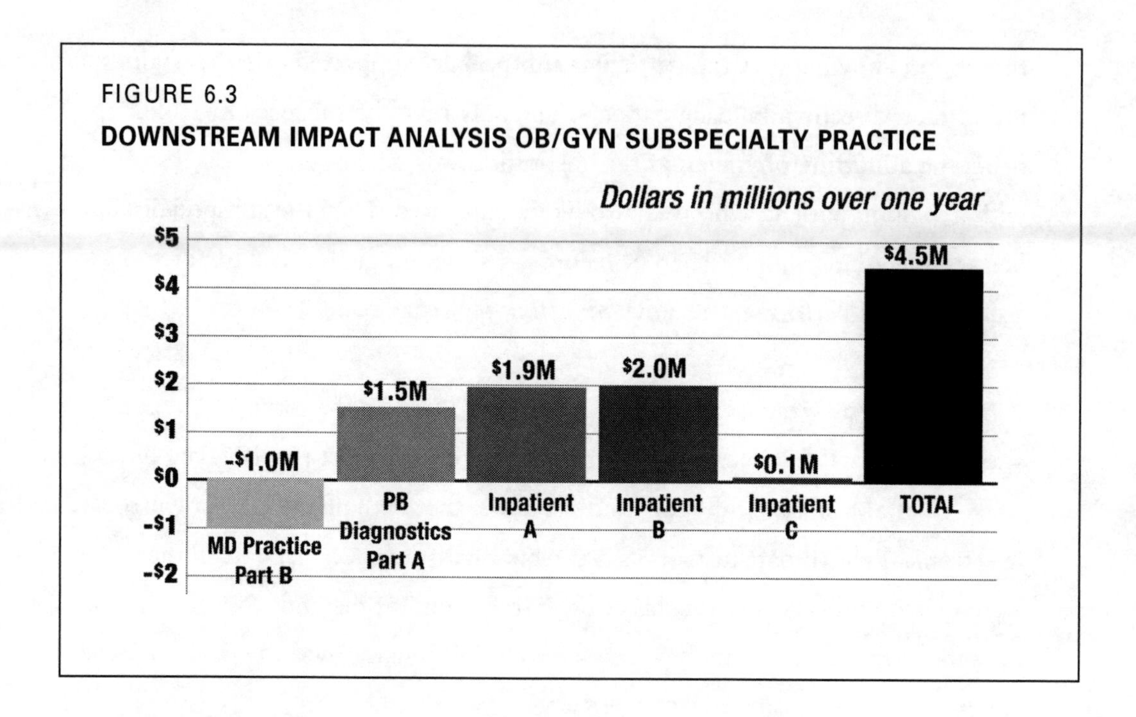

FIGURE 6.3
DOWNSTREAM IMPACT ANALYSIS OB/GYN SUBSPECIALTY PRACTICE

Performing downstream analysis

First of all, make it easy on yourself. Start with already available measures recognized by finance, marketing, or other departments. Use the outcome measures your organization already recognizes as important. That is also much easier than starting from the process up because the databases will already exist. The first time is always the hardest—particularly when you need to come up with a rationale for subjective attribution. Practice makes perfect, and once you get it right, just keep on repeating the report.

Service line executives can also access marketing and planning databases, finance, human resources, professional market research (not your own)—whatever is needed to measure the impact.

Another big recommendation is to buddy up. Work with finance. If you don't like their data, work with them to understand it and fix it.

Some rules that will bolster your credibility from the start include the following:

- Make sure that you use, and quote, the departments who have the most credibility regarding the data you used. Particularly at first, they will likely be asked to confirm the data. Make sure they know what is coming and are on board with your analysis and findings.
- Always source your data back to the original departments.
- Quote their data, not yours.

SUMMARY: DOWNSTREAM ANALYSIS RECOMMENDATIONS FOR BEGINNERS

- Keep it simple. As you gain experience, go for more complex analyses. Don't get stalled out early by focusing on something complex. This is particularly true if you're working with finance for the first time. Take the time to establish trust over a simple problem.

- Put together project partners who can help you—in finance, business planning, marketing, or other applicable departments. Think ahead to report acceptance—leverage their credibility to establish yours.

- Determine baseline data and contact activity for whatever you are measuring, from a new clinical program to a marketing campaign. For instance, if you are considering a new annual event, perhaps downstream measurement will include clinical contacts by women who were targeted or attended the event and had not used the health system within the prior two years.

- Determine how downstream results will be measured. New inpatient or outpatient cases? Physician visits? A reduction in high-cost, unnecessary utilization?

- Establish a start point and a time frame for counting activity. The suggested clinical contact is 24 months after the program starts.

- Agree with your documentation partners on the method to determine incremental portion of downstream activity due to this activity. (This is the subjective attribution previously discussed.)

- Determine what type of financial or other measures will be used to calculate return on investment and make the appropriate information available.

- And have hope: EHRs will make downstream analysis far easier than it is now.

What Women Want: Attracting the Female Consumer

We have talked about being market-driven, not product-driven. That's always been a rule for success—and will be even more so in an ACO environment.

The successful women's health service line executive will provide the customer with information that she doesn't know she doesn't know, which leads to services that exceed the customer's expectations. Adding that "DKDK" category is what defines the A-level experience. Anyone can tell a customer what she already knows and what she knows she doesn't know. That's C quality. And A is where you want to be.

The basic rule of market-driven program development and presentation is to first find out what you're doing that you should be doing, what you're doing that really shouldn't be happening, and what's missing. Don't trust your instinct for that.

A classic example of a bad mix between market-driven and product-driven thinking is all too often prenatal classes. Boomer women, who pretty much invented real childbirth education back in the 1970s, form the bulk of nurses today. Nurses in their 50s will be a quarter of the RN population by 2012. Because they are the dominant age group in nursing, many of them teach childbirth preparation and courses that haven't changed substantially since they started teaching them years ago. Add today's Gen X and Gen Y mothers and fathers into the mix, and there is often a huge mismatch of perspectives and educational tactics.

Another mismatch is in urogynecology and pelvic floor disease. The magic that is coming out of this specialty is outpacing itself every year. There is a significant gap between what is being offered in most communities for women, and what could be offered—the "don't know don't know" factor.

Great providers and great care teams create successful consumer experiences and generate word of mouth about your organization. However, a very small percentage of your total market comes through your door every year. And most experienced marketers will tell you that word of mouth, alone, takes about a decade to change perceptions, and we already know that perceptions of brand are what lead to incremental volumes. Marketing-focused executives can change perception very quickly—sometimes over the period of one year or so, depending on the size of the market. Consistent marketing can shift market share very quickly when combined with great programs.

Marketing is an art beyond just advertisements. PR plays a huge part in successful marketing. Because it takes more skill and management than simply placing ads, PR sometimes doesn't get the support it needs. Be thankful if you have PR support at your organization. And if you don't—particularly in women's services—you might want to consider contracting outside the organization.

This is not a how-to section on marketing. That's a whole book by itself, and there are outstanding books available on the topic. This section will add to your background on female consumers and tell you how to leverage marketing.

The power of market research

I am a huge advocate of market research. Particularly for the IDS-level executive, it's the only real way to know what your market is thinking. Even when you maintain clinical contact with patients, you still don't know the needs of the women who do not come to you—and you have to know that before you can claim their loyalty. Without that knowledge, you can be speaking to the choir. It's those who are *not* using you that you need to know about.

Objective, quantitative research about your market is critical to your planning process. Much of this is already available at your hospital or health system, although it may take a bit of work to uncover. Although I constantly hear that data are not available within XYZ health system, I usually find they are. Discovering where the data reside and what they can do for your specific service line is the challenge.

State and national databases are there, as well as brand surveys. So are DRG and other utilization databases. Demographics are commonly available, both for current and future populations, and are greatly enhanced and simplified by mapping software. If you can't access one database, you can likely find it through a colleague or by buying into that database for a specific purpose. And Google has more information than can even be imagined.

Databases reside in different places in different organizations. Sometimes the database is in finance—even when it doesn't seem like financial information. Most often, you will find the databases you need for planning in your business planning and development arm. Health systems also have a wealth of quantitative data on patient satisfaction and usually on physician satisfaction—indicators you should be watching. You will want to spend some time getting to know these databases and how they can be queried or manipulated to serve your specific purposes.

Because of the wealth of objective data usually available, additional market surveys are not usually required for program definition. However, if you do need a large market survey for some reason, consider online surveys, which save money and—particularly with childbearing-age women—are easily done.

Most of the time when you are building or revising programs you will want qualitative market research, which is best accomplished through focus groups or focused interviews, either in private or group settings. Quantitative data tells you "what." Qualitative answers the questions of "why" and "how"—details critical to new program development and implementation. The primary questions explored in qualitative research usually revolve around the good, the bad, and the missing: what healthcare is doing in your area that is good, what healthcare is doing that it shouldn't be, and what is missing for the consumer.

One of the most powerful aspects of qualitative research is a powerful resonance with clinicians. Trained to be suspicious of (clinical) quantitative research, physician, nurses, and other key staff always relate well to focus groups in which they participate. Those are real patients, with real concerns, talking about their experiences. One solid anecdote during a focus group can shift approaches and attitudes overnight. With focus groups, make sure you take maximum advantage of the research: Invite clinicians to watch from an observation room and use the opportunity to build your team. While you will usually have a video, it's never the same as being there, and never viewed with as much interest as the live group will be.

Many market research and marketing firms are now focusing on the patient experience, which is a different and very useful way of approaching market research. This research is fundamentally market-driven and supports the matrix organization, following the patient through every touch during her experience. Topics cover the complete range of services she experiences and lend validity to key consumer issues that may have been dismissed in the past as irrelevant.

How do you know when it's time for qualitative research? Here are suggested times:

- At least every five years for baseline services
- Before you start a new program
- Any time you need to test an investment of long-term significance to the organization
- When you can't get the data you need from satisfaction surveys.
- When there is a persistent organizational question about the needs of the consumer
- When you want to lay the groundwork for significant organizational redevelopment

- When you have tackled all the basic elements of quality and organization of care, and it's time to get to a new program level
- When your marketing team says so

Leveraging psychographics

This is where planning for your population starts to be fun. Demographic information includes just about any kind of statistical analysis of a population. The census is a great example. You'll find data about gender, age, ethnicity, marital status, and so on. Your business development and planning staffs have huge amounts of additional demographic information, sometimes right down to the ZIP code level, everything from income levels to where childbearing-age women will live 10 years from now.

These are great numbers that can paint a pretty clear picture. It's still from your perspective, though. You are the one looking through the glass. You won't get a feel for your consumers' thoughts from numbers alone.

Psychographics bring demographics alive. These descriptions paint a picture of customer attitudes, beliefs, and values. You can get to psychographics from demographics; there are many purchasable databases that will provide demographics with a psychographic overlay. These are usually accompanied by colorful descriptions of the populations in the area you are studying. Those descriptions paint an immediate picture, much more than demographics alone. A term like "empty nesters," for instance, gives you a faster picture of a neighborhood than demographics alone.

That gets closer to "feeling" your population and where they live. We're dealing with women health services through a lifetime, and psychographics should play a key role in how you develop programs and particularly in how you market to women.

Generations last about 22 years, so there are about six generations of women alive today:

- The G.I. Generation: 1901–1924
- The Silent Generation: 1925–1946
- The Baby Boom Generation ("boomers"): 1946–1964
- Gen X: 1964–1980
- Gen Y (New Millennials): 1980–2000
- Digital Natives: 2000 on

Authors William Strauss and Neil Howe maintain that the same four generations repeat themselves every century, as do the events that create the characteristics of every generation. If you want to think a decade ahead, they have great clues, and the history to back up their theories.

If you really want to tailor your marketing so the message is clear to your target female populations, become a student of psychographics. One message does not work for all women. Boomers and seniors like thoughtful exploration of new ideas; Generations X and Y want bullet points with optional links for more information. Boomer women are the fastest growing psychographic in social media, but Gen X and particularly Gen Y already live there. If you aren't there, too, you just don't exist.

As for that nine-year-old you know, she has been linked to the digital world almost from birth. The rest of us might as well be reading old parchments by candlelight compared to the information access she already has. If you want a taste of what she will have at her fingertips, spend a few minutes with her on her iPad™. Try an iPad application called Xe—The Elements, by Theodore Gray. Compare it to how you learned (or didn't learn) the periodic table. Consider how early in her life, and how quickly, she will have the periodic table figured out compared to how you managed it. We're talking light years of difference—even compared to Gen Y. That's why you need a great marketing team, so they can figure all that out and tell you what to do.

DOS AND DON'TS WHEN MARKETING WOMEN'S HEALTH

Dos

- **DO** build a team that you can trust, and take its advice. Question the team until their strategies and tactics make sense to you, but take their advice.
- **DO** measure marketing results, but spend your time on the big picture, not the small picture. Establish some internal benchmarks for performance, for example, a minimum of 75 attendees to justify marketing a seminar and asking physicians to come speak. Fine-tune to get there. However, what's most important is making the brand needle jump and increasing volumes, particularly incremental volumes—not just churning old patients for new.
- **DO** use marketing to prod clinical or business product development. The promise of marketing can bring an interdisciplinary team to the conclusion of its project much more quickly. Likewise, the threat to withhold marketing—which you should use very sparingly—can occasionally help you get over operational barriers.
- **DO** check with legal first on regulatory issues before you start marketing voluntary physician staff.
- **DO** use marketing to bolster specific needs in margin or volume. It's not always just about brand. You can focus on marketing aimed at improving margin by focusing for a while on high-margin services. Just don't get it out of proportion in the long run.
- **DO** ensure that you are absolutely consistent in the use of your brand. If McDonalds used 20 different logos or icons, you wouldn't instantly recognize the golden arches for what they represent. If you don't do the same thing, you're losing millions of opportunities every year to reinforce your brand.
- **DO** meet with your marketing team regularly and do market consistently. Consistency is the key to brand visibility. Periodic marketing doesn't do it, especially in obstetrics where your families are in and out of that phase in four years. You need to be highly visible during that short period. Word of mouth might never reach them, particulary in highly mobile regions.
- **DO** figure out how to leverage the power of PR.
- **DO** use multichannel marketing—traditional and new media. Traditional media has its role in every generation, but if you're not present in new media for Gen Y and under, you don't exist. If your marketing team doesn't have anyone who can tell you exactly how to use social

DOS AND DON'TS WHEN MARKETING WOMEN'S HEALTH (CONT.)

media and online marketing, do fill that gap quickly—from Generation X down to digital natives. You're spending too much money if you are only doing traditional media. And the switch isn't easy for marketing firms to make; it's an entirely different approach. Just add someone to the team who never did traditional marketing, and you'll get where you need to be.

Don'ts

- Like finance, you **DON'T** have to come from a master's degree in marketing to lead a marketing team and use it well.
- **DON'T** wait to market until you have a perfect product. You never will. And if you can't find something positive to market now, one of two situations is happening: Either you're an "act" person who never gets anything stabilized—you can't market until a product is stable enough to name and make promises about it—or you don't know your product. Every woman's service line always has something excellent you can market once you start thinking like a consumer. If it isn't facilities, it will likely be staff or an exciting program. Get out there; don't wait for perfection.
- **DON'T** be afraid to stop a campaign, or any other tactic, for a good reason. Every organization has months where marketing is pulled to make a bottom line (usually at the end of a fiscal year), and everyone has failed events, sponsorships, and campaigns. Be smart; don't put marketing above the well-being of your organization or your service line.
- **DON'T** think advertising alone equals marketing.
- Finally, **DON'T** ever, ever give up your brand, or sublimate it to another brand. There are marketing packages you can buy for women's or for OB. Most manage to feature their name prominently; some have very appealing names. Although it's tempting to buy a package and let it roll, if you feature someone else's brand or byline, you are marketing that brand, not yours. If you buy a marketing package, use their logo or byline only when you are contractually required to do so, and do so in the smallest icon or font you can. Remember, the minute you stop buying the package, your competitor will (sometimes before if you're dealing with a national competitor with a presence in your area). That means if you featured the national package, you marketed for your competitor. Protect your brand; don't build someone else's.

At the end of the day, remember that women are smart and they don't like false advertising. Make sure your product delivers what you promise; don't get ahead of yourself and promise the world. Women are savvy consumers; how you speak to them and what you deliver will establish a strong loyalty bond. Treasure it; it's your brand.

Your marketing team

Just as everyone is a closet architect or interior designer, everyone is a marketer. Whatever your background, with all its nuances and specializations, marketing is a specialty with at least as many subspecialty areas as yours.

How you handle marketing will drive a lot of your success, so plan carefully now to access the advice of these professionals. My own service line marketing team has met every two to four weeks for nine years, and it's always the most fun I have each month. If you want to relax and laugh, marketing is where you can consistently find that—creative types are not easily constrained.

Our team is an incredible group that includes service line staff who keep separate eyes on each of our three areas of responsibility (women's, obstetrics, and children's services). We have—for a seven-hospital system—two terrific lead public relations specialists; one internal and one external, both shared with other service lines. Yes, there are men on the team, two brave souls who add balance and more than their fair share of humor. We have fabulous media buy expertise, social media gurus, Web geeks, geo-marketers, multichannel marketing geniuses, and creative staff hidden away in strangely decorated caves who somehow come up to our ever-increasing challenges.

And none of them are full-time marketing for our service line. It's a great matrix team. Control of their FTEs isn't important; what's important is that they constitute a terrific team, totally focused on our service line when they are with us. They advise in all things marketing, and we owe them much of our success.

Having this kind of support can only make you look good. Choose your team carefully. As you should do with all interdisciplinary teams in your service line, think inclusively. Pay particular attention to getting expertise in areas in which you have little or no background. If you're a boomer, that's probably social media. If you're a Gen Xer, you probably think 50 is old, so you need someone to tell you about boomers. Either way, use the team well to balance your knowledge about how to access and talk with your market. With women, communication is everything.

Rule of three

There are dozens of potential markets in women's health. Once you consider psychographics, ethnicity, and the ways marketing is becoming tailored to specific populations. It is helpful to know you don't need to do everything to make an impact in women's health. You can't—no one can do everything. Women's health is too broad and too deep.

I've long had a rule of three: If you become well-known in three broad areas of women's health, you will likely dominate the market. Choose where you want to focus and do it well. In a world of complexity, focus is what will keep you on track to accomplish your objectives.

Summary

- There are probably more "delicious distractions" in women's services than in any other service line. You will have more opportunities presented to you for investment of resources than you can possibly imagine.

- A construct of brand, volumes, and margin can help focus your activities. That construct can help you align your service line goals with those of the organization. Define and measure the value of your service line, and direct your budget, energy, and time.

- Because much financial analysis is still driven by departmental thinking, downstream analysis of value is critical to service line success, which spans time and processes. Investments in one department can show return on investment in a completely separate area. You will need to build a team of analysts who can help you demonstrate that value.

- Within the same construct of brand, volumes, and margin, it is important to focus marketing activities and build a team that can advise you on meeting the needs of the diverse population of women in your market, as different from each other as is possible in six living generations.

- Focusing on becoming the best in your market in three broad areas of women's health will likely yield market dominance.

- Protect and elevate your brand; make it strong and keep it there.

References

Bevolo, Chris A. *A Marketer's Guide to Measuring Results: Prove the Impact of New Media and Traditional Healthcare Marketing Efforts.* HealthLeaders Media, 2010.

Buerhaus, Peter, Staiger, Douglas O., and Auerbach, David I. *The Future of the Nursing Workforce in the United States: Data, Trends and Implications.* Jones & Bartlett, 2009.

Children's National Medical Center. "Telemedicine Applications in Pediatric Cardiology." *www.atmeda.org/news/2005_presentations.*

Corrigan, Karen. *The Complete Guide to Service Line Marketing,* HealthLeaders Media, 2010.

Strauss, William, and Howe, Neil. *Generations: The History of America's Future, 1584 to 2069.* HarperCollins, 1992.

CHAPTER 7

Kicking Off Your Service Line

Whether you are kicking off a new service line, converting from hospital-centric to integrated delivery system (IDS), putting a new emphasis on either obstetrics or women's, or fine-tuning your position, you will want to follow the project stages to make sure you complete each stage and create alignment on your goals (see Figure 5.1 in Chapter 5).

Critical Components of Successful Women's Services

It's easy to get lost in marketing and even easier to get focused on a new or renovated facility. There is absolutely a place for both. If you have the best quality and programs in your area and no one knows it, you will have a problem. Women are concerned about facility issues, although those concerns tend to be around safety (think parking and illumination), access, cleanliness, privacy, your ability to act in an emergency (hallway clutter), and comfort. Those are not necessarily guaranteed by a new facility—and many very successful programs are in old facilities. But everyone loves new, and there is definitely a point at which your facility can fight against your competitiveness.

However, your success in the long run will not come from either facility or marketing, but from a category called "people, programs, and processes" (see Figure 7.1). This is the one that will carry you through when you don't have capital and at times when you have to pull marketing. This is where the real foundation is in women's health, and 60% of your success, according to market research with more than 10,000 women of all ages.

FIGURE 7.1
CRITICAL COMPONENTS—SUCCESSFUL PROGRAMS

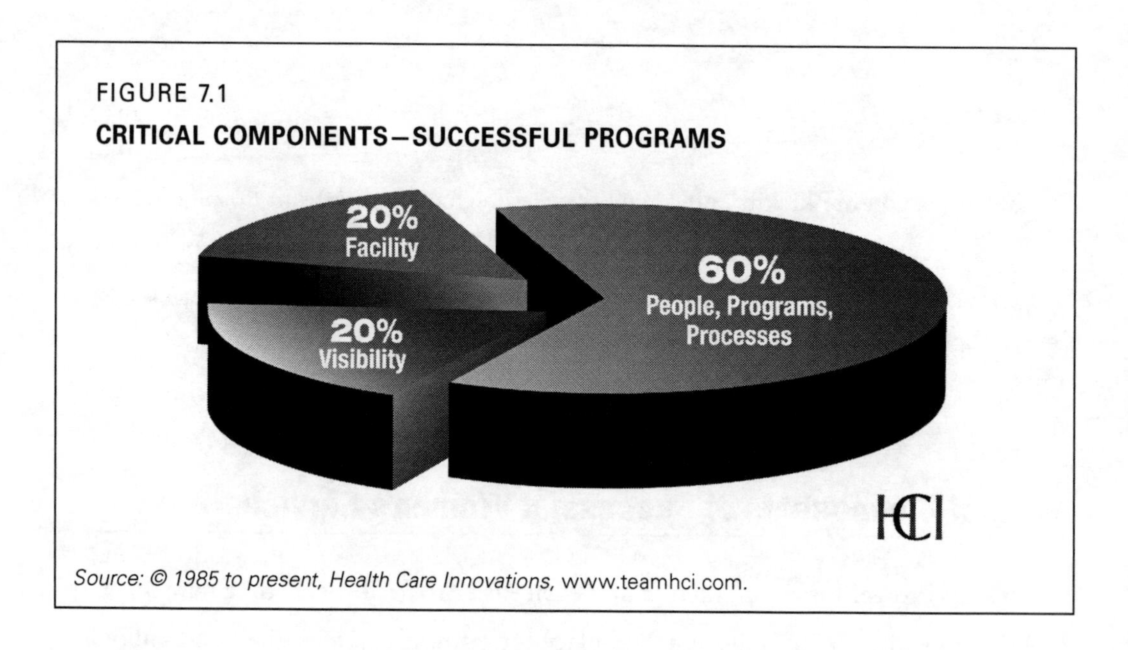

Source: © 1985 to present, Health Care Innovations, www.teamhci.com.

People, programs, and processes

What's in this category? Your depth and breadth of physicians and other providers, to start with. By and large, women go to physicians and other providers first—not hospitals. Those of us within hospitals and health systems like to think they come for us, but unless you have your own insurance plan, they don't. Even if it is coverage that drives some to you, you likely still can't depend on "captive" insureds alone to meet your volumes—and that leads back to your providers very quickly.

In addition to your providers, your programs are in this category—high-quality programs that get named "the best" by outside groups, or little-known market-driven or interdisciplinary gems you make public. Think of your prenatal and women's educational programs and outreach, remembering that women are attracted to healthcare information. Think of your multidisciplinary programs that provide comprehensive breast or gynecology-oncology care, not just surgery—or a gestational diabetes management program, not just a nutritionist with a diet plan.

Your processes also play a key role—for example, how easy it is for a Gen Y woman to register for classes online? How is she helped to be successful with lactation? There are very few things that a woman does that a man can't, and these define her as a woman at a time she is the most vulnerable. Birthing and breast-feeding are two of those key challenges. How do your processes ensure she feels successful and confident—no matter how the birth or breast-feeding experiences turn out? It's not a method of how she delivers the baby or how she nourishes her child, but whether she feels successful. That's a completely separate process.

We are fortunate in women's health in that we often have more licenses to nurture the emotional needs of our customers. Take full advantage of this. Use patient experience-enhancing initiatives within your services. However, everyone has emotional needs, no matter how tough they seem. Every diagnosis is a challenge. Don't forget to leverage your experience to help your organization ensure that all patients—women's health, orthopedics, or oncology—have the same care experience you want for your service line.

Likewise, actively support organizationwide initiatives like the quest for the Magnet Recognition Program®, which creates a nursing leadership and culture that guarantees outstanding care. From experience consultants to performance engineers, whatever lifts the organization will impact your service line and customers as well.

Bon Secours Virginia Health System put 11,000 employees through Ritz-Carlton® service experience training—everyone from senior leadership to physicians and all levels of staff from housekeeping to food staff. The difference in the patient care experience systemwide was astounding, although the initiative was greeted at first with cynicism by many. Patient satisfaction will increase as well with each of these initiatives.

In the end, it's still how you're cared for as a human being that often matters the most—and that comes from people, programs, and processes, not bricks and marketing. Own your people, processes and programs, and work the matrix to make sure you like what you see, hear, and feel.

Defining your goals

We now have two concepts that provide general focus: the relative importance of people, programs, and processes for overall success; and the three categories in which you plan and measure your success: brand, volumes, and margin.

Using Figure 7.1 can help you take an honest look at your strengths and weaknesses. Talk to others. If you're just starting in service line, take the first one to two months to examine existing databases and interview your operational, medical, nursing, and departmental leaders. Ask them to identify the good, the bad, and the missing—from their perspective—within your women's service line.

Ask every woman you meet—your waitress, someone in line with you, people at parties—where they are getting their healthcare, who their physicians and other providers are, and which hospitals they use. Check your organization's overall brand among women. When I started at Bon Secours, every pregnant woman I met told me she was going to deliver at a competitor hospital. I made it my goal to change that, and we did. Now they all talk about one of our hospitals, and I rarely hear about the competitors. That's a nice informal reflection of our market share data, but it gives me far more information about how we are really doing than looking at the data alone.

However, you should put a time limit on how long you spend collecting your initial data, both quantitative and qualitative. Once you start to kick off your service line, you'll likely need more formalized research.

From the interviews and informal information gathering, start a list of your general strengths and weaknesses. Divide them into facility-related, marketing, or the category of people, programs, and processes. Now it's time for a first look at opportunities. Note low-hanging fruit. Consider how those opportunities blend with the organization's focus, where the two merge. That should be where you focus your first efforts.

You'll want to go back to your drawing board for significant challenges, but you will also want to leverage your opportunities quickly.

Getting focused

Remember that in Figure 6.1, brand builds market share, which builds margin. But you can start at any part of the diagram. So, for your first effort, what do you need to move first? Are volumes solid? If not, how can you immediately improve those? Are you comfortable with margins? Do you have capacity constraints but still need to improve margin? Focus on how you could leverage high-margin patients without stretching capacity to help the organization. If you're invisible in the marketplace, consider how you will change that—a longer plan than just a year, but one you have to start to see results next year or the year after. Don't wait for the ideal time; it won't happen.

Once you sort out where your focus needs to be, the next step is to work backward into what actions will create the change you need, which should then drive your marketing and business development efforts. If it's volumes you need for a new service, it's time to develop a small project team to determine the barriers and take advantage of opportunities—both internal and external. Go back to the basics of market-driven organizations: Determine where the market share will come from, the access points, and what the messages should be at the access points—obviously including referral sources. Launch a physician introduction plan, which should be at least as focused on physician lounge and office activities as advertising. Figuring this out is where your finance, business development, legal, and marketing colleagues are invaluable resources to you.

For everything you consider doing, ask where it will play out in brand, market share, or margin. Now is the time to make sure that the tactics you are considering match your objectives.

Finally, make sure you have thought ahead to how your impact will be reported. Review the standard reports the organization already does. Make sure what you are doing will show up there. If not, do your own report—but validate that you're not getting too far out from the norm before you dream up all-new methods.

Keeping score

Keeping score helps everyone. "If you can't measure and report it, did you really do it?" is the service line equivalent of "If a tree falls in the forest and no one hears it, does it make a sound?"

Scorecards are a great way to keep you focused and to regularly report what you are accomplishing. Some organizations report key data themselves. An example is quarterly reporting on market share from the entire organization down to the service line level. There are usually reports on patient and physician satisfaction, or image and visibility surveys. Finance is usually reported regularly, and will include both your own service line and other departments; you may be receiving some matrix-based reporting as well. Some organizations report key indicators every day throughout the entire organization, everything from gross patient revenues to births to inpatient and outpatient activity.

You can probably access physician activity reports pretty quickly as well. Data are usually easily obtained, whether traditional or new media was used.

In most organizations today, plenty of information is being reported. So you may not need anything more than an occasional checkup on key indicators specific to your service line. However, scorecards enable you to keep track of the pulse of the service line and prioritize where your focus should be. If you do design a scorecard, the following are some categories and tips:

- Before you add to the report barrage, make sure what you're looking for isn't already in some other report. Avoid report duplication.
- Try very hard to get any separate report set up electronically, linked automatically to already-available data, so that your report populates without human intervention. Most organizations are close to this in our digital age and getting closer every day with EHRs. Setting up this kind of report is a one-time process, and then it runs automatically. If you're the first in your organization to do this, consider hiring from outside to set it up.
- Consider how often you will really use the data. Quarterly is enough for most reports; anything more frequent can show heart-accelerating changes that may well not hold. I avoid looking at births, for instance, more than twice a month. The variability is too great for more frequent analysis.
- You will likely want a separate report card for obstetrics-neonatal, and for non-obstetrical women's services.

- For each scorecard you develop, you will likely want some mix of the following, likely by unit and combined. The data should be presented graphically whenever possible, and as year to date, same quarter last year, and the last full fiscal year:
  - Volumes and average daily census
  - Acuity
  - Outpatient activity
  - Key quality indicators
  - Gross revenues (to which you can mentally apply a ratio that estimates margin)
  - Payer mix
  - Patient satisfaction by unit
  - Provider activity—additions and changes in privilege status or volumes
  - Disposition at discharge

  I haven't included patient or physician satisfaction because it is usually measured less frequently than quarterly, but you may want to include it in the last fiscal year of data.

- For overall women's services, you might want to key in on those that are critical to the organization—usually those of the other service lines.
  - Percent of female patients in other service lines you are supporting, e.g., heart or cancer. If you and your service line colleagues are doing your jobs, the percentage of female patients in those services may not increase in relationship to male but you definitely do not want to see the percentage of women fall.
  - Watch key clinical quality indicators by gender, not just the total male and female population.

The change process

If you are anything like me, at any point you likely see literally dozens of areas where you could make improvements. Take a deep breath; there is a lot to be said for incremental progress. Build on strengths and handle the challenges over time. We are often moving massive organizations. Change does not—and should not—happen overnight. Be patient. Be objective. And respect the change process.

Particularly in the matrix model, everything you do will have ramifications in other departments. Some change you will lead, some you can lead with a partner, and some will be led around you regardless of whether you like it.

There are different types of experts who assist organizations during times of change. Your boss should be your first recourse, and human resources can be a huge help. Organizational development professionals are to be cherished. So is help from Six Sigma–type process leaders, human factor professionals, and productivity engineers.

Only you will know when to ask for help with change, but here are some tips. Ask for help—either from your boss, a peer not having the same conflict, or the change professionals—when you run into consistent barriers with people or departments focused on process. That can be any functional department in your organization, such as some of the more linear departments I have mentioned, or operations, or clinical units.

Remember: Once outcomes are introduced to a group that is focused on process, there is always conflict at some level. Most of healthcare is a process; service line is what links those disparate pieces together to achieve an outcome.

During times of significant change, the best context I can recommend is a modification of Elisabeth Kübler-Ross' famous stages of death and dying (see Figure 7.2). Any significant change follows exactly the same steps, with excitement following acceptance since we are talking about change after all, not death.

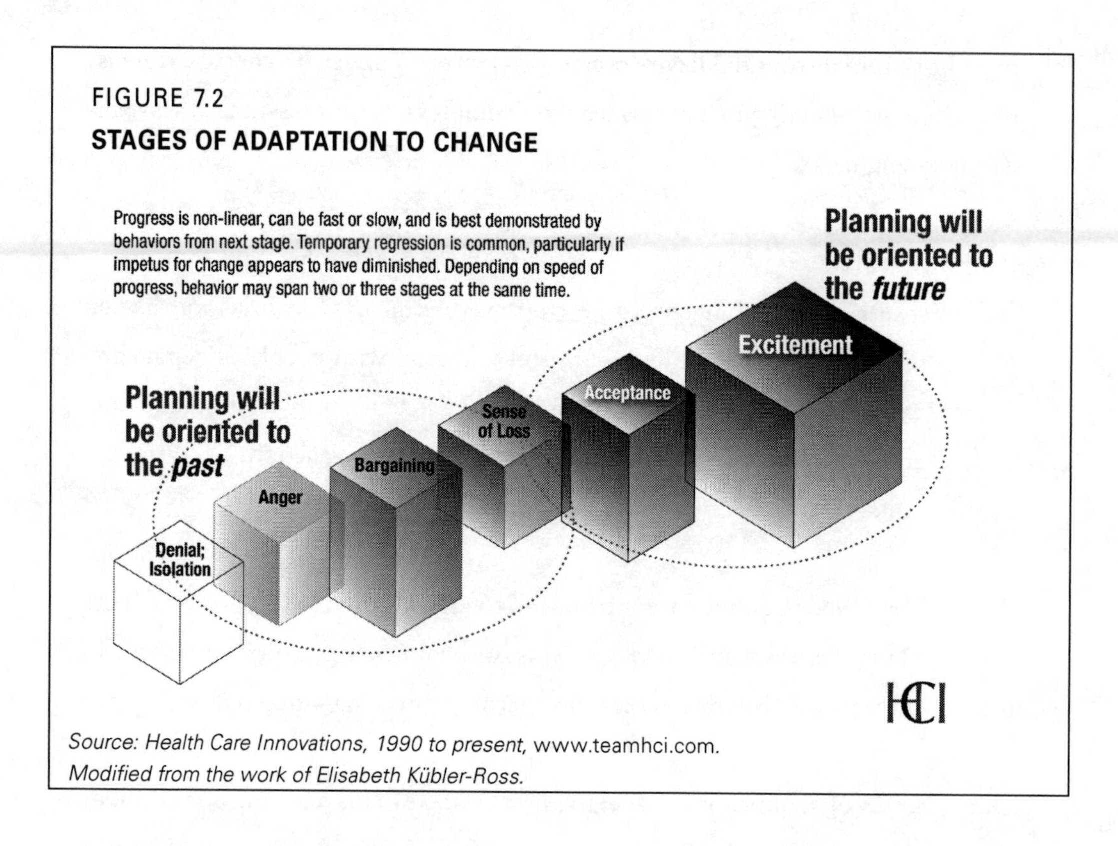

FIGURE 7.2
STAGES OF ADAPTATION TO CHANGE

Source: Health Care Innovations, 1990 to present, www.teamhci.com.
Modified from the work of Elisabeth Kübler-Ross.

A key point in this diagram is that planning will always be oriented to the past until those dealing with the change are at least in acceptance of the change. While the first stages of denial, anger, bargaining, and sense of loss can be pretty traumatic, moving through these stages is absolutely critical before future-oriented planning can occur. Only data and information will move smart people through these stages.

When you are going through a significant change process, my advice is to hang this diagram on your wall and refer to it often. You will see the processes happening over and over. Having this context can ease the process, particularly as you go through anger. I tell people anger is a good sign—it means you have at least broken through denial, unfortunately, it's often a distinction of dubious reassurance.

Also use this diagram to reassure others about the change process. Clinically trained staff relate easily to this context. Change is always difficult—and the bigger the change, the more difficult it will be. Have empathy for those going through it, but keep clear about the context and the stages. Doing so adds some often-welcome objectivity to the process.

Launching Your Service Line

Whether you are kicking off a new service line or planning to take your service line to the next level, use the stages of projects (Figure 5.1), which will always help you navigate the waves of change. In particular, starting (and staying) at "act" is not a good way to lead successful change over the long run. If you use the stages well, change and stabilization will happen naturally.

Even if you are not starting a service line or engineering a major change, you want to stick to some format of the project stages every year just to keep on track. That process may be internal or involve your expanded group of stakeholders, including providers and staff. Particularly as you move from a hospital-centric to an IDS model, or if you merge with or absorb another system, you will want to conduct formal planning on a regular basis with those who make you successful. Your opportunities to hear directly from them will become more limited, and your providers and staff are the ones who will make the service line successful. This process is useful for you, as well as for them.

The kickoff

There is nothing like a retreat to say something new is happening, or to excite and motivate your providers and staff. I prefer the term "future search," as it has a better mental image for me. The future search as an inclusive strategic planning process can propel organizations into cohesive action through cooperative planning. Within healthcare, a future search is often compressed to a day and a half to optimize the participation of providers. It's our challenge to work hard before and after to maximize their time with us.

Whatever your scope, organizing these events is a significant project. There are several critical pieces that need to be pulled together before, during, and after retreats to make them successful. A planning period of at least three months is critical. I've been in the consulting world for a while, so I admit to having a bias, but I believe there are two key roles that should be played by outsiders during a retreat:

- I highly recommend you hire a skilled **facilitator.** This is a priceless role, and you'll only need it this once. Don't get a beginner and don't be afraid to give up control. Also, don't be afraid to go outside the organization. Although you may have terrific, professional facilitators within your organizational development department, if they are also involved in staff coaching, you may want to get someone from outside just to assure staff of objectivity.

A great facilitator will guide you as you put together data for participants, help you plan who should attend, and—above all—be able to manage the retreat processes *and* get to the desired outcome. Many will also help you reduce the findings into an outline for your implementation plan.

Make sure you check references and feel comfortable with your facilitator because he or she is absolutely critical to the process. You will be working hand-in-hand with them; you need to have great communication and be on the same page regarding expected outcomes. Then give up control and let them do their job.

- The other great place to involve an outsider is as a **content expert.** You may want more than one. You can definitely plan the content within your institution, and you, personally, could deliver it. But there will likely be more than a few individuals going through denial during that content presentation. Often it is just better to have an outsider deliver the news. Then there are two of you saying it's the right way to go, not just you. And it's always a delight to let someone who can fly out the next day take the brunt of anger about change; that's a great role for consultants, and good ones will understand that it's part of their job.

  Don't be afraid to give up control of content delivery. You can sit back and learn yourself, and you will come out with new insights. Even if you already knew 90% of what you hear, you will hear it at a new level. You can also model lifelong learning for your staff, and get to spend time with them as a participant. It's a rare opportunity.

> Think tanks with expertise in women's health will have experts you can bring in to deliver an update— and you can find experts in specific areas easily by researching recent conference speakers. Take full advantage of the both clinical and strategic learning during your future search or retreat and offer CME and CEU credits for clinical staff.
>
> If you are focused on just OB-neonatal, or solely gynecology, you can likely put together a set of internal experts. (Comprehensive women's health would likely require an internal panel too large to be time-effective.) If you use a panel, you will need to very actively manage their presentations so you get to your goal. You'll need a lot of coordination time up front. Remember: Don't expect outcomes from process-oriented speakers, so be careful whom you ask, and make sure you get where you want to go by the end.

With a narrow enough scope, it's possible you may find content experts who are also facilitators, but it's unusual; each requires a different skill set, and each needs to be sensitive about presenting data not recommendations (content experts) and where facilitation can start to become direction (facilitators). Outsiders never have the same perspective you and your stakeholders will have about what will work for your organization in your region. Let them present data and information and opinions, noted as such. Then it's your job—leaning on your leadership teams—to determine the ultimate direction.

If you use the format of a retreat, make sure you use the opportunity well. If it's important enough, get everyone away from work. Many organizations now pay voluntary (not IDS-employed) providers to participate within a legal framework, and medical groups give relative value unit credit for participation or otherwise recognize employed provider participation. And make sure you use the opportunity for interaction well—a great social event, with or without a speaker, can greatly facilitate retreat interactions and relationships.

Retreats are great kickoffs when things are going well or for routine change. Every once in a while, you find a service that is truly in trouble, either from a cultural perspective or simply because a decade or two passed it by, and the whole service needs to quickly be brought into a very different era or culture. This doesn't happen very often, but when it does, it shares project characteristics with something else that doesn't happen very often—the opportunity to build a woman's hospital. Surprisingly, the steps are the same for both situations. One is fortunate enough to have a new facility to focus on, whereas the other involves different building blocks—those of the culture of the organization. However, both need the same visioning, planning, action, shaping, and stabilization. One uses an architect, and the other depends more heavily on organizational change professionals.

CASE STUDY

Change agent

Sue Korth, BSN, PhD, had the challenge of opening a brand-new women's hospital. As vice president and chief operating officer of Methodist Women's Hospital in Omaha, NE, she wanted providers and staff to join her in her vision of raising the bar for women's healthcare for Omaha.

Korth embarked on a process that formally redefined the mission, vision, and values of the new women's service, and then went to work on creating the ideal patient experience and culture for female patients. To bring home the new culture, she required staff at the existing hospital to reinterview for all positions at the new women's hospital. Some were brought along, but others found a better fit elsewhere.

Before, during, and after opening, Korth used intensive daily leadership huddles, weekly unit meetings, an online newsletter (Korth's Korner), and weekly unit rounds. She ensured an open-door policy. She made sure the leadership team and staff knew they had permission to challenge and change decisions as much as possible so staff owned the processes. She also made sure her peers across the IDS knew and agreed with what she was doing.

She made the physicians and staff part of every decision. Although she was predominantly talking about architectural and flow decisions, the process isn't any different if you are dealing with significant culture change and organizational development staff.

Korth lit their fire with what clinicians need to get excited about change—the prospect of becoming a top 10 hospital in the United States for birthing. That promise provided both the "what's in it for me" motivation and the opportunity to make a true difference in Omaha. Both types of goals are critical to motivate clinical staff.

CASE STUDY

Change agent (cont.)

Korth employed the following tactics to build a new culture:

- Develop a picture of where staff and care can be—not just where it is now.
- Develop a careful plan for the facility and the culture change process.
- Remove the silos. Great outcomes are a team process, not separate departmental processes. Break down staff barriers, name and position barriers—every barrier you find to creating a unified team.
- Develop customer service skills—a new cultural vision. "You can build a brand-new building, but without customer service, you have nothing," Korth says. "It isn't your problem, it's our problem."
- Launch with care and a lot of hands-on attention. Make sure you have the structures in place that support the need for quick adjustments. Stay with the adjustment process until you are sure it's taking off on its own. "Don't take processes that are not working with you and expect the processes to change automatically. Change the processes first," Korth says.
- Stabilize the new processes. Make sure they are part of staff recruitment, orientation, and evaluations. Make sure the vision is carried out in policies and procedures, and in the experience of patients, physicians, and staff.

Proactive alignment process

Alignment does not occur on its own. Clinicians come from a history of competitiveness about "the best way" to achieve results. Make sure you provide data to them in the best possible way to create alignment. That will often be the opposite of the way business data are otherwise presented. When you're creating alignment with business colleagues or with clinicians, use the format familiar to them.

Business presentations often start out with recommendations, then go back and explain the data, a "this is what I want to do and why" format. That works for those who come from a business education or background. However, this is also the quickest method to ensure resistance from clinicians, who were taught an understandably ordered approach of collecting the data before coming to a diagnosis and plan. Every clinician has had a nursing or medical student who spent 10 minutes with a patient and came to the conclusion of a brain tumor or something equally off the wall. Good clinicians know that, in non-emergencies, you carefully explore all the data first, and then draw your conclusion and plan.

You also have data clinicians have often never seen before, which is even more reason to carefully present information that has been part of your thinking for a long time. The same rule holds true for everyone outside your service line. The reason you're on board is because you know the most about your service line. Even if something seems incredibly obvious to you, make sure you pull it out if it's a key part of a recommended change.

This really is just being market-driven. Speak to the market's needs, not from your own perspective (which would be product-driven in this case). Walk in their shoes.

Consider the issue from their perspective. Present it that way and you will prevent a lot of unnecessary angst.

The keys to alignment

There are four keys to establishing alignment:

1. Make sure you present **objective and well-balanced data.** In the field of market research, researchers refer to "happy-ending research"—research that happily proves what the sponsor thought in the beginning. Much of your data will likely have a happy ending just because you know your field—not because you biased the research to get there. There will be other findings that surprise you, and there are bound to be findings you didn't expect and may not welcome with open arms.

   Everyone with whom you work on a regular basis will be aware of your biases and beliefs, and smart people always look for biased findings, whether intended or not. One of the best things you can do for your career is to present data objectively. If you have a bias, say so—particularly when the research you present doesn't support that bias. Make sure you are not pushing your own agenda. Over time, people will trust your data more because they know you are objective. That will shorten the time from presentation to action.

2. A second key is **listening.** We're all racing to an objective, pedaling faster than ever before. It's important to take a breath and really listen. You work with smart people; ask their opinions. When you are on a mission to create alignment, it's even more important to ask opinions and really

listen. If you do it right, you will accomplish three goals at once: building trust, learning more about how stakeholders are interpreting your goal and tactics, and creating a better program.

"It's absolutely critical to let physicians and staff members know you are listening, that they are being heard. You won't necessarily be able to do everything they want, but you heard them, you considered their concerns, and will do what you can," says Korth.

A wise friend in my organization taught me early on that the best sign I needed a vacation was when I found myself becoming agitated at the failure of others to see where we should be heading. It's good advice.

3. The third key is taking time to develop a **relationship**—the only way to build trust. As soon as new initiatives are proposed, there is a tendency to get going immediately and set up structures to achieve the goal. That's important—you don't want to plan so long that the opportunity escapes you. But particularly when providers and health systems are being tossed by turbulence, it's time to make sure you have trust with those upon whom you depend for the success of your initiatives. The barriers of time and distance will become more difficult as your IDS grows—use every means of communication you can find to stay on the same page with the leaders of your organization.

4. Finally, one of the most important variables in creating alignment is **motivation.** If you, your staff, and your providers are forced by the

> economy into dealing with finances from morning until dark, it's sometimes hard to remember that at least 90% of those people with whom you work did not go into healthcare just to make money.
>
> Clinical staff in particular, and many administrators, went into healthcare believing they could make a difference. Particularly in these days of economic free fall, it is critical to remember that. Money may pay the bills, but it's not a motivator for these clinicians—a fact that's easy to forget.

The steps to motivation are really pretty simple. Take the time to set up an honest relationship. Then speak to the immediate opportunity for the organization and for the clinicians—the "what's in it for me" factor. Next, take the very critical step for everyone: How the proposed change will contribute to better health for women, and why it's the right thing to do from a far larger perspective than any immediate benefit to the organization or to them. Then—and only then—follow up with the call to action. If you follow these four steps, you will find gaining alignment is much easier than you might think. Honest acknowledgment and relationship. Immediate opportunity. The greater possibility. The requested action.

Physicians and the E Words (Engage and/or Employ)

During the past decade, decreased reimbursement has forced physicians to be smarter about management of their practices. Many larger groups formed in part as a response to economic realities. Some physicians enrolled in MHA or MBA programs, and that lifted the general business knowledge of practices.

Younger physicians—Gen X and particularly Gen Y—want a life, not just a practice. They said a firm "no" to the older model of joining a practice at a very low salary until they earned their stripes. In that model, older partners made more money, partly from the work of new members of the group. Today's young physicians want to be paid now for what they produce, and the old tactic of buying a practice doesn't interest them either. The goals of young physicians have significantly changed recruiting, succession, and retirement planning of smaller groups and solo practices in particular, another cause of stress for these groups. Gen X and Gen Y are attracted more to larger groups with guarantees of fewer call nights.

Clinical practice has changed dramatically in the last two decades. For OB/GYNs, the old standby of a mature practice—hysterectomies—disappeared long ago. Today, OB/GYNs are delivering babies much later in their lives, rather than retiring into gynecology only as was the case in earlier decades. For some, it is because they genuinely love it. For others, it is the easiest way to increase revenue to pay college bills and fund retirement.

That plan held together fairly well for boomer OB/GYNs until the recession hit in 2007. At that point, their retirement plans took a substantial hit at the same time births fell precipitously. The pressure on OB/GYN practices nationally is substantial right now, and service line leaders need to approach them with empathy. The contract under which today's boomer OB/GYN entered the specialty is broken—anger is very close to the surface among many of these physicians and among small groups and solo practitioners.

Even before the Patient Protection and Affordable Care Act and accountable care organization discussions (which demand that healthcare systems and physicians work together), physicians and hospitals were being drawn together for strength and to avoid many of the increasing legal barriers to some older business arrangements.

Patients go to physicians before they come to hospitals, and hospitals and systems have many zeroes behind them. It's an obvious marriage, but it is full of tumult as both groups learn to work with each other.

When and how you get into physician employment will be driven by the model you are using for physician alignment. Figure 7.3 shows the range of business arrangements between hospitals and physicians today.

FIGURE 7.3
HOSPITAL-PHYSICIAN ALIGNMENT MODELS

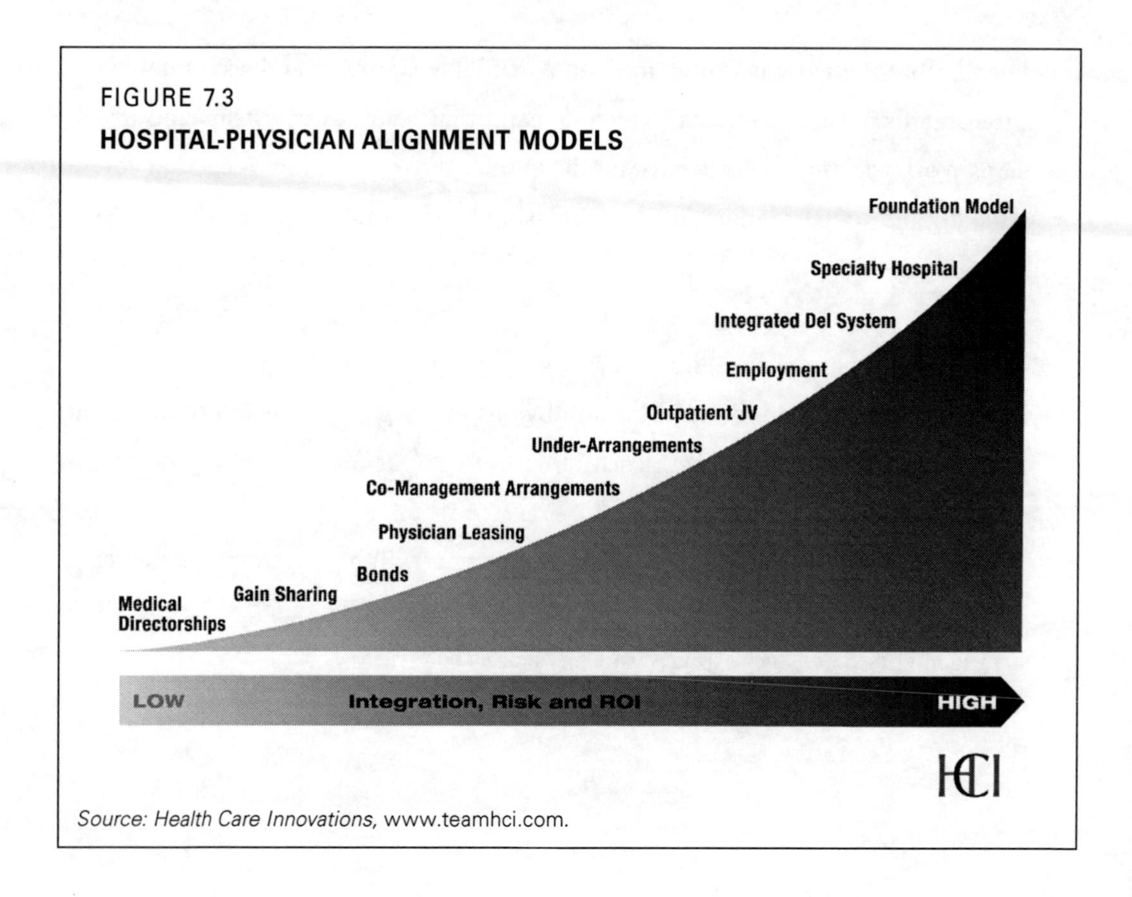

Source: Health Care Innovations, www.teamhci.com.

Each model has its advantages and disadvantages. The least integrated business model is on the left, and that is the one with which most readers will be familiar—the medical director model. This model simply hasn't yielded the clinical or business outcomes needed today.

The most integrated is on the far right, the foundation model, in which a foundation runs all the operations of the entity—whether inpatient, outpatient, physician, or hospital. The oldest of these are the multispecialty clinics such as The Mayo Clinic.

Most hospitals and systems today have experimented extensively on the left side of the table. In the past five years, employment has picked up substantially in all areas of the country, as well.

You may or may not be looking at physician employment, and if you are, you may be looking at a particular segment, such as primary care or perhaps subspecialists. Even within the same IDS, strategies vary among geographic divisions or service lines. You may already have enough private OB/GYNs to care for all your births in one market without destabilizing the market by employment, and in another division have an almost 100% employment environment.

The strategy for physician alignment and employment varies among service lines. For instance, it takes fewer orthopods and cardiologists to provide care for a given population than it does family practitioners, OB/GYNs, internists, or pediatricians. And at the top of the specialty pyramid, it takes very, very few subspecialists to care for a given population.

Working from the top down—the target population—it's not difficult to estimate the number of physicians needed. The average number of deliveries per year, per physician, is about 125, with significant variation on both the low and high ends. That's quite a bit fewer than it was 10 years ago, reflecting the maturing boomer, the lifestyle-dominant Gen X segments, and the dominance in residencies of young women who, at the end of the day, are still "the mom."

You can calculate how many physicians you need for your target obstetrical population. It's the working back to how you will align with those providers in a win-win relationship that gets interesting. Issues of market saturation and destabilization come up quickly if you are in a predominantly private practice area, with the impact of the recession creating a fiercely competitive arena. Every action has a reaction.

Whether you are looking at OB/GYNs, internists, or family practitioners, the employment decision is a complex one and will require leaders to reflect on the goals of your organization. Make sure you get a rough idea of how many physicians you will need to be aligned with your strategy. For women's service line leaders, it's not just numbers, either. The first physicians to jump on board with hospitals have often been those at the peak (or after the peak) of their earning capacity. You may find that most of your organization's employed physicians are 50- to 65-year-old males. Many residencies—not just OB/GYN residencies—are now 50%–90% female. If your employed physicians are predominantly male, your women's service line will have a competitive issue. So watch and inform medical group decisions carefully to make sure your organization stays well balanced and represents the age, gender, and ethnic diversity desired by women, and likely men, today.

Another contextual issue is the percentage of providers in your area who will actually be employed versus in private practice. In some areas, most physicians are already employed. Those are predominantly in areas of the country where multispecialty group practices already had strong roots, like the Midwest. In many other areas of the country, private practice—albeit larger groups—still dominates. In some parts of the country, IDS physician employment may not ever reach more than about 10% of the total physicians required to maintain and grow market share, improve quality, and innovate for the future.

In all the excitement about physician employment, make sure you don't take your eye off the ball: Keep your provider relations strong with the other 90% who will not be employed and who can practice wherever their needs and the needs of their families are best met—your voluntary physician staff. Explore what their needs are; see how you can fill them. What works for them will usually work for you and your organization. Meet. Talk together frequently. Make sure your staff are meeting with them.

In women's specialties—in and outside of OB/GYN—consider a physician advisory council, with both employed and private physicians. Look for physicians with organizational altruism who truly are committed to women's health and working with you. As you strengthen your non-obstetrical program offerings in particular, that's where your greatest challenges—and strengths will be.

Everyone likes to be important, and everyone likes to be part of decision-making. You won't always be able to make every physician happy, but the more you exhibit fairness, transparency, and keep relationships strong, the better able you will be to weather the turbulence ahead.

Summary

- Although it's easier to think about new facilities or marketing, the truth is that your long-term success will depend on people, programs, and processes. The care and nurturing of these is probably your most important job.
- To bring people along to new programs and processes, they will need data—both clinical and business. Your organization likely already has many available databases and reports; some of the types of data you and your staff will need are listed in this chapter.
- Regardless of executive data and reporting, the heart of your service line is your providers—both voluntary and employed—and clinical staff. To achieve your objectives—and to keep them excited about what they are doing—you will want to involve them regularly in both data sharing and planning. There are multiple ways to do this—one method discussed is a periodic future search.
- Whether you are just starting a service line, moving it to the next level, or just want to stay in touch with your clinicians—the heart of your service line—this format provides the learning, excitement, and alignment you will need. Done correctly, it ensures your stakeholders have the same information as you do and will therefore be most likely to come to conclusions both of you will like. This format allows them and you to plan together; you can hear their feedback, which will strengthen your plan.

- Use the opportunity carefully; it will be expensive in terms of participant time and energy, so you want to make sure you are well prepared. Although we haven't talked much about consultants prior to this, engaging outstanding facilitation and content expert assistance may add objectivity, neutralize resistance, and ensure that new ideas are heard more completely and in a least threatening environment.

- Regardless of alignment efforts, these are turbulent times for both hospitals and providers. Be aware of the pressure on providers, and be alert to changes in practices, which can affect your bottom line. As your hospital or health system develops its formal business physician alignment strategy, make sure you know what your position needs to be to ensure your goals, and that you are an active participant in planning provider alignment.

CHAPTER 8

Staying On Top

In this book, we looked at the external and internal environment affecting the healthcare industry. We examined all the reasons the complex organizational design we call "service line" exists and is growing, and we looked at the myriad vectors inside and outside of healthcare that are breaking down traditional silos and refocusing processes on achieving measurable, safe, satisfying outcomes.

We talked about how a women's service line is critical not just for obstetrics and gynecology, but to draw in the female healthcare gatekeeper for the entire extended family, from parents to spouse and children. We even talked about why the men's service line may really be the women's service line.

We looked at the exciting—and sometimes threatening—changes taking place in healthcare in general, and specific to women's services. All women's services, for women ages nine to 109, include new opportunities in gender-based programs, for example. We talked about the importance of the service line maturing from a hospital-centric model to supporting the integrated delivery system (IDS) model.

And we added a new task for the women's service line in an accountable care organization (ACO) environment: leveraging the power of the family healthcare gatekeeper to help providers achieve the ACO goal of care coordination—a job she is already doing.

We defined your customers and ways to reach them. We looked at a construct for sorting out what's important and what isn't, honing your focus to achieve your goals and those of your organization. We identified ways of using finance without getting lost in it. And we talked about marketing and the need to fine-tune the message to the customer, particularly considering the unique psychographics of the generations with whom you communicate in women's health.

We looked at project stages, whether the project is something as complex as starting a service line, changing a culture, or building a new hospital—or as simple as developing a new program. We identified customer groups—both external and internal—and talked about becoming market-driven versus product driven, and about managing the matrix.

We listed the characteristics of service line leaders and how to effectively handle resistance and build alignment. We talked about the change process—how to categorize anger and negotiation—so you have a context for it outside of yourself. This is a process you will want to respect. Keep the stages of adaptation to change close by and refer to it often during moments of stress.

We leaned on authorities from several disciplines, and talked about when it's smart to get outside help, as well as, how to use the many resources already inside your hospital or health system. About the only authority we haven't covered is you, and what's valuable to you while building or growing a women's health service line.

Maintaining a Healthy Balance

The first and last rule of success as a service line leader is knowing and taking care of yourself. You will be juggling multiple demands from every possible internal and external customer. You're the one who has to take care of you.

Talk to other service line leaders and find out how they maintain balance. Carve out time for yourself. Get that car with the fabulous sound system to lighten the burden of constant IDS-wide trips. Figure out how to add on a concert or a massage or a game of tennis at the front or back end of that overnight trip to the far reaches of your IDS. Plot how to steal your spouse or best friend away for one of those trips and extend it to a weekend. Play.

Make sure you find your job rewarding. If you're too exhausted, you won't. Take care of your perspective—you are the only one who can do so. Perspectives need to be nourished like anything else. Identify what your mind does when you're really tired, and when you see that happening, make sure you take time off.

Surprisingly, your hospital or health system will get along just fine while you're gone. The last thing you want, for your own sanity, is that it doesn't, so build in the systems that stabilize what you're doing, and let others be part of your team.

In short:

- Know and take care of yourself
- Know your customers—internal and external
- Know your market
- Know your organization
- Respect the change process

Jamie Babbitts is just one year into her new role as the first women's service line leader for a three-hospital IDS in northeastern Wisconsin that forms the eastern region of Hospital Sisters Health Care System. I asked her what the five most important lessons were that she learned during the year. The following are her insights and advice:

1. **The value of focus.** "There is so much to be accomplished, and so much going on in healthcare right now," Babbitts says. So she focuses on the one thing that she wants to accomplish each quarter in order to stay on track.

2. **The need for a great team.** Service line leaders need to put together a strong team with the right mix of expertise because you won't have the time to learn everything, says Babbitts. "As you move up, you're moving beyond your competencies and experience, entering new areas of expertise you haven't dealt with before. Yes, you could stop to learn

all the functions you don't already know, but there simply isn't time. You have to trust and not get so caught up in the details that you can't get anything done."

3. **Find a way to engage physicians so they support you when you make hard decisions.** Leverage all your physicians, because when they buy in, whatever you are trying to accomplish really takes off, she says. "It's critical to take the time to get to know and trust your physician leaders, and give them the opportunity to get to know and trust you."

   The same is true for your business colleagues, Babbitts says. "It's not so much a matter of trust with them as getting to know what each can or cannot do and learning to work with each to get on the same page."

4. **The need for patient persistence.** "Don't back off your goals and what you should be doing," advises Babbitts. Service line leaders should listen, fine-tune as needed, and persist. It is important not to react to the last thing you or a colleague heard. Put it in the context of reacting to change and move on. "You really need leaders with that backbone; they support you over the difficult times. Return the favor," she says.

5. **Appreciate your mentors.** Babbitts' mentors include:

   - Her direct supervisor, whom she has known for years and is "someone you can vent to, and know it's safe ... someone who gives you the confidence to take risks, and understands the human element involved in everything you do," Babbitts says.

- A woman of wisdom—someone who is outside her department, but still in healthcare. Someone with a lot of experience, but who doesn't tell you what to do. "A mentor who can offer feedback, perspective, and the confidence you will figure it out," Babbitts says.
- Another women's health service line leader. Babbitts found service line–specific weekly coaching from a consultant outside the system who is more experienced in women's service line development. Within women's services and leadership, "a coach adds context, focus, perspective, and support," she says.
- Community mentors. Having someone who can open doors in the community for you can be advantageous. "There are times in your life when you can take advantage of this type of mentoring, and times when you can't. Having someone do that out of the goodness of their heart can add so much to your career; it's something we all need to do for each other," says Babbitts.

One more bit of wisdom: Find people at work who can make you laugh, says Babbitts. "If you can't laugh at work, it's going to be a long life."

